MW00606450

BEND THE WILLOW

A story of family, friendship and love

By Le Lieu Browne

Book layout and cover design by Jonathon Wolfer
www.thelonewolfer.com

IN MEMORY

My beloved mother, ***Nguyen thi Le****, my role model, for her tenacity and sacrifice in raising seven small children by herself.*

My beloved father, ***Huynh van Tet*** *(though his life was cut short), for his spiritual influence on me.*

My beloved husband, ***Malcolm W. Browne****, for our wonderful life together.*

FOREWORD

Le Lieu Browne's story is one of the power of love even in the tragedy of war: First, the lifelong love of a daughter for a father who had been cruelly taken from her at an early age. And later, the love of her life, the legendary American journalist and Vietnam war correspondent Malcolm W. Browne.

Born in the southern part of Vietnam when it was a French colony, Le Lieu Browne was a small child when Japanese soldiers occupied it after the French defeat in World War II. When the war ended, Vietnamese communist guerrillas kept fighting to try to keep the French from coming back. They killed her father because they took him for a French sympathizer.

The family broke up, and Le Lieu was sent with a cousin to France and England while, at home, Ho Chi Minh's forces defeated the French, and Vietnam split in two in 1954, the communist North and the American-supported South, where she returned in 1960 to work in the government press office in Saigon. There, the following year, she met her future husband, then a correspondent for the Associated Press, and her life changed forever. Browne's prizewinning photograph of a Buddhist monk's self-immolation in protest against the corrupt and intolerant Ngo Dinh Diem regime in 1963 became a symbol of the problems that continued to plague the South Vietnamese cause even after Diem was killed in a coup encouraged by the United States. Browne shared a Pulitzer Prize for his coverage of the conflict in 1964. A few years later, with hundreds of thousands of American troops intensifying the war, Browne and Le Lieu were married, and he joined The New York Times. They returned to Southeast Asia and helped cover the defeat of South Vietnam and its absorption in 1975 into the communist regime in the north, the Democratic Republic of Vietnam.

Here, in Le Lieu Browne's words, is life and death in Vietnam as most Americans have never seen it before, seen through the eyes of a South Vietnamese woman who understood the fatal flaws of both sides of the war. Here also she recounts her and Malcolm's later adventures in foreign reporting posts from Asia to the Balkans to South America. And, finally, she tells the heartbreaking story of coming home with her husband to the United States to care for him until his death in 2012 from complications of Parkinson's disease. Read this book to be inspired and uplifted by the power of the human spirit even in the face of terrible adversity.

--Craig R. Whitney

PREFACE

The Viet Nam War has lately been in the news – Ken Burns's documenary film "The Viet Nam War," and several books recounting the blight of war y former FBI agents, Viet Nam veterans and Vietnamese refugees and victims ave brought back that period.

My memoir is partly about my childhood in Viet Nam, but it is mostly ocused on one specific era that had shaped my whole life. It started at the be-inning of the 1960s and ended around 1980.

My name is Le Lieu Browne. I was born in Viet Nam, and became a aturalized American through my marriage with Malcolm W. Browne, former Bureau Chief of the Associated Press in Viet Nam, and former foreign corre-pondent with the New York Times.

Malcolm and his friend David Halberstam of The New York Times ointly won the Pulitzer Prize in 1964 for "…their individual reporting of the Viet Nam war and the overthrow of the Diem regime."

Malcolm was also the recipient of the World Press Photo award in 1963 or his iconic photograph of the "burning Buddhist Monk," which provoked hock within the Kennedy administration and finally caused the downfall of South Vietnamese President Ngo Dinh Diem and the Nhu brothers. As a for-ign correspondent with the New York Times, Malcolm covered South Amer-ca, the India/Pakistan war, Afghanistan, Eastern Europe and South East Asia.

Malcolm died on August 27th 2012. Going through his files and pa-ers, I was suddenly drawn back to the most tumultuous and unpredictable xperiences imprinted in my memory.

Those began with the early 1960s, before I met Malcolm. That initiat-d unexpected and almost miraculous life changes that involved fate, intuition, nd a lot of luck --an emotional journey that flashed back and forth from my hildhood to the present time. This journey and the lack of certain childhood xperiences had molded me into a woman of determination and independence.

As I began to write, old wounds and painful yearnings began to sur-ace, mingling the present and the past. I had gone through my teenage years without a male role model in the family. In France and in England, I was left lone to decide my own orientation. I felt deprived of my father's love and amily support.

At that time, my mother was singly raising seven children after my father's disappearance. He was kidnapped and killed by the so-called Viet Minh, the communist guerrillas in the south at that time. My mother was a teacher in elementary school. With her meager salary, she was forced to sell family plots of land to send me and my two elder brothers to France. The schools in Viet Nam in the 1940s were constantly interrupted by leftist student demonstrations. I was never close to my two brothers whose sole interests were outside of the family circle.

After a decade studying in France and England, I was asked to go back to help my mother with my two young teenage brothers who were at difficult crossroads in their educations.

I was 23 years-old, without any experience except being a student. I had applied for a job with the South Vietnamese Ministry of Information and was accepted. I was like a young tree in its prime, transplanted to another place with a different climate and a different environment.

Having lived in free countries growing up, I was suddenly thrust into the authoritarian world that I had first escaped. I did not fit into Vietnamese society, facing male domination, gossipmongers and old traditionalists.

I instantly chose to find my own path. That path was mystic, frightening, and yet enchanting to me. Naïve, immature, and defiant, I let an invisible hand guide my unsteady steps. Then I thought of my mother who had suffered discrimination in school, being a single defenseless woman. Not being religious, I nevertheless believed in spiritual power, that of my dead father guiding us all along.

With a lost childhood, longing for paternal guidance, drowning in a sea of doom and uncertainty, I was just a mixed up kid. Then I met Malcolm and love began to bloom. The childhood memories intertwined with the womanhood adventures to end up on a happy note.

The story did not end there. Being married to a foreign correspondent, I shared with Malcolm an exciting life, travelling all over the world, meeting celebrities and heads of governments. In my past, I had never dreamt of such an incredible life. It was a dream worth holding onto. I, therefore, determined not to stay home or to bear children. Instead, I began to learn news photography and to write travel articles to contribute some small earnings that would permit me to travel with Malcolm. Most importantly, Malcolm and I were, in my eyes, a unique and inseparable couple.

This is our story.

Bend the willou
Sharpen the blou
Bend the willou
Enlighten the life
Bend the willou
Nurture
Indulge its blows.

CHAPTER ONE

The FedEx man arrived as scheduled. He had been at my house before, a young 5ft-5-tall man with a smile on his face as he walked in with a ready-prepared envelope. He was ready to receive a letter when I took him to the room and showed him the 22 boxes ready to be shipped.

"Oh I didn't expect such a load!" he exclaimed," let me go out to see if all these will fit in my truck." He quickly stepped out on the porch and immediately returned with a smile. "Yes, it's ok."

Without further comment, he carried each out to the van. Watching him going back and forth with the boxes, somehow I felt as if I was watching Malcolm's body being carried away again and again. That thought drew me back to so many painful memories of the past, when Malcolm's Parkinson's Disease was going from worse to worst. His balance was unstable and his mental state was unsteady. How many times I had had to follow behind the stretcher on which Malcolm's inert body was lying. And finally August 27, 2012 in the evening, the last journey, when the ambulance came to carry his listless body to the Dartmouth Hitchcock Hospital. The last one was vividly imprinted in my brain and will be there until I die.

"Well, it turned out that all the boxes fit ok in the van," the young man said, drawing me back to the present. I watched him driving away with those boxes, Malcolm's whole body of work, to be collected for the Library of Congress. I put on my sneakers and walked to his grave on the hill of our property.

"I hope that you approve what I have done with your archives," I told him. During his illness, Malcolm never mentioned or discussed with me what to do with his archives. Being too preoccupied with his health, I put everything else on the back-burner. I was too weak to dare bringing up any subject that might relate to death, for fear of being accused of wishing him dead. I was often confronted with that question, so many times, whenever we had some quarrel concerning his health.

At the end, I was left with scattered boxes containing documents, articles, letters and photographs of his whole career.

I was aware that Malcolm's archives would be a priceless trove to be preserved for historical research. The Associated Press, which sent Malcolm to Viet Nam and with which he always had a special relationship right up to his death, acquired a small collection of his work during his first five years of covering the Viet Nam war, as the AP's Bureau Chief. With no idea of how to process the main bulk of his collection, I browsed through his files, hoping to find some clues or correspondence from any institutions that might have written to him.

By accident, I encountered our good friend Neil Sheehan, who covered Viet Nam in the same period for the United Press International wire service. During our conversation, Neil mentioned the Library of Congress and even kindly offered to introduce me to the right person there. I felt lucky and bewildered at how my life had turned out to be full of serendipity and unpredicted discoveries. I was like a tumble-weed, blowing in the wind in no particular direction. For 50 years, living with Malcolm, I depended on him to make decisions on almost everything that was important to him. When I first met him and he learned about my father's fate, he tenderly told me that he could protect me in place of my father. Now he is gone and I have to fend for myself. I should be proud to say that I have made it.

Left alone, I thought that I could fend for myself as I had done throughout my single life before marrying Malcolm. I was young and had a whole future in front of me. Married life had spoiled me and turned me into a 'sissy'. Now with age, any slight difficulty seemed like a mound of worries that I had to confront, sapping all my strength for days.

I began to learn the ropes, and the first, most important thing I learned was to appreciate the kindness and generosity of friends. From one friend to the next, I have achieved the task of transferring Malcolm's archives to a most prestigious institution. And so his wishes (I hope it was what he wished) were executed.

For the whole summer, I had been going through his files, sorting out what to let go and what to take out. File after file had set off acute emotions and memories of the past. There were things that I already knew and others, many others, filled me with excitement, nostalgia, admiration and painful surprise.

For days, I relived the past, and at the same time I realized that I had stepped into unknown territory that had so far been hidden from my life. The man with whom I had shared my life for the past half-century suddenly appeared, to my eyes, as a different man. I still could detect kindness, care for privacy, consideration for his family and friends and generosity to others. But rage, despair, mockery, disillusionment, loneliness, and other extreme emotions he had kept inside were spilled out in his personal notes, letters to the editors and his enemies. Many times, I had to stop reading his dispatches and control my own emotions, my own loneliness and my sorrows. I was haunted by his unhappiness and yearned to take him in my arms to apologize for my past ignorance. Some other times, I accused him of betraying my love. I almost had a nervous breakdown.

"I had a rich life," Malcolm reflected about his past during his illness. "Everybody dies sooner or later. So there is nothing to say."

I did have a good life thanks to him. It has been a dream life that I had never imagined I would live.

"Luck is an eliminable part of the human condition…However are we victims of serendipity; skill, choice, prudence, and a moral compass all have the roles in the game of life." [Luck, the Brilliant Roundness of Everyday Life, by Nicholas Rescher.] Could that apply to me?

I met Malcolm in November of 1961, a week after an attempted coup against Ngo Dinh Diem and his government. I vividly remembered how one afternoon, coming out of my office and hailing a cyclo to go home, I happened to glance at the pedestrians pouring out of the buildings, I saw a tall white man walking along with John Griffin, an AP correspondent whom I went out with from time to time.

"I'll see him soon," I thought, glancing at Malcolm as the cyclo sped up through traffic. He was tall, very thin, wearing a white shirt and Khaki pants, with a cigarette in his mouth. His young white face and blond hair gave an appearance of an Englishman. He seemed to be awkward and slightly limping next to John Griffin.

I already knew that he was going to replace Griffin, who told me in advance that he was going back to the USA because his young daughter had developed cancer. Malcolm and John were in deep conversation, paying no attention to the crowds of Vietnamese coming out of their offices. His tall stature and incredibly white skin made him stand out among them. He was different from other Westerners whose tanned skin betrayed their frequent outdoor exposure.

"Is he going to ask me for a date?" I was smiling to myself. I had met and sometimes dated a lot of foreign correspondents in that period. With most of them it was just friendship and professional. Still, it was regarded in

Viet Nam as daring, or even louche, behaving like a bar-girl, because women from good families would never degrade their reputation by going out with foreigners.

I was lonely and alienated among my own people. Being abroad for the whole decade, and recently repatriated, I felt more at ease with Westerners, speaking their language and adopting their culture. I had lost touch with the Vietnamese way of life and barely got along with Vietnamese men. I cared less about my reputation. As for being a representative of the government offices, I supposed I should be more discreet, but on the other hand, I considered going out with the press was good for public relations. Whatever, I didn't care.

By the time I had come back to Viet Nam in 1960, I thought I was in another country. I was struck by the change in my family. They were all adults now, and thrilled to have me back. The first few days, I was very uncomfortable with the surroundings. I had problems adjusting to the heat, to the way of life in the countryside where my family lived, to the outhouse, common shower and most of all to no privacy. My mother's friends came to greet me mostly out of curiosity, and my mother proudly brought out her best china to treat them with all kinds of Vietnamese delicacies.

I was recalled to Viet Nam because my mother could no longer support my living in Europe. In addition, my two youngest teenage brothers were in high school in Saigon, and my mother, who was a teacher in our home town, could no longer pay their rent and school expenses there. My sister, who was married to a Frenchman and was the mother of two toddlers, lived in Saigon. She tried to help the family whenever she could afford to.

After a few days in our home town, I had to go to Saigon and to report to the Information Office. Nobody had mentioned to me that we had an apartment in Saigon, until we arrived at the destination. I was appalled as soon as I stepped into it -- an empty studio, a square room of 15ft by 15ft, my brothers' home. It had no furniture, not even a chair. We ate on the floor and slept together on the floor. A small electric hotplate was used to cook our meals. That's where I had to live while going to work. I tried not to say anything to offend my mother, but my heart sank with pain and despair. My mother had to pawn my meager jewelry to feed us until I cashed my first salary.

To make myself a little privacy, I bought some curtains to spring across the walls within a small space big enough to fit a single mattress on the floor as my bed. All my clothes were hung on the same string and I rouched inside to do my daily toilet. The bathroom was at the end of the all, shared by all the tenants living on that floor. I had heard so much about lums in Europe, and now I lived in one.

The room was on the walk-up fourth floor. The building was located n a small alley surrounded by other small buildings in the center of Saigon. t blended in with them with the same grey color, the color of a century of lirt, grime and grease. The place was noisy 24/7, with street vendors outside ur window combined with traffic, babies' cries, children playing, and family arguments. I didn't realize how poor my family was.

My first plan was to make enough money as soon as I could to move out of that insidious place. I reported for my new job at the Ministry of Information. The minister interviewed me and gave me a week to settle down. When I learned about my salary, I was in such a state of mind that without the support of my mother, I might have committed some insane act. It was a salary for slaves, in my mind. How could I afford to move out of that lum? There was no way for me to afford any decent place to live for at least several months. I could not stay in that room without blowing my brains out. My mother and my sister took pity on me, and every week, my mother ought and prepared food at home and carried it up to Saigon to feed us so o avoid my having to do any cooking. My sister made her own contribution y bringing extra food from her home and cooking for us on the hotplate.

One day, my brother came to my office and told me that there was cottage not too far from the center for rent. It was a one-story cottage behind the owner's house, with a big separate kitchen, separate bathroom, and separate toilet. We even had some space in front of the cottage to park bicycles and hang laundry. There was a small living room, enough to fit two single beds for my brothers and a dining space for our meals and the whole loor upstairs. The rent was affordable on my salary.

I was so exhilarated that I and my brother immediately went to the bank to withdraw all my savings to pay the deposit and a month's rent in advance. We moved in over the week-end. I had my private bedroom upstairs. t was paradise. The place was in a quiet residential area and the market was n walking distance. Now, my mother had a decent bed to sleep in whenever she came in. My sister and her kids could share the meals with us any time. could even have guests for dinner. My salary barely paid for all the expenses, but we were all happy. I began to get used to the heat, the humdrum of ife, with constant traffic flowing outside. I got reacquainted with my family, ppreciated their support and understanding. They gave me energy and inspiration to carry on in my inconsequential job.

I had started not knowing quite what to do.

Thinking back on my situation, I was amazed that somehow some mystical or magical power had steered me in the right direction. It worked in a mysterious way that somehow things turned out to my benefit. I had a roof over my head, a job – the first that fell into my lap. I had no clue what the future reserved for me and did not lose any sleep over it. Despite my sadness of leaving a good carefree life in Europe, I began to believe that it was a good move for me to come back and to learn to live a real life in my native surroundings.

I recalled the agony of the last few months in Paris.

When I was asked to come back to Viet Nam, my mother had no money to pay for an airplane ticket. My cousin, whom I had gone to France with, was married to a medical doctor, a very devoted Vietnamese nationalist. As soon as he graduated from the Medical School in Paris, he promptly moved his family back to Viet Nam. During these years in France, I had sometimes depended on my cousin to help me out when I was having trouble. Now, I was left alone in Paris with no resources but to depend on the generosity of my Vietnamese boyfriend while I waited for the Vietnamese government to accept my visa application. I had met Gia, my boyfriend, while we were studying English in London. We were thrown together because we both were lonely in that big city, speaking poor English. I was 21 years old and had always avoided being involved with any man romantically.

Growing up with five brothers who did not carry a lot of weight in my life and gave my mother more trouble than comfort, I had no trust in men, marriage or love. I was involved with Gia more by convenience and self-interest. He was 25 years old and lived with support from his wealthy parents. He sincerely loved me and provided me with the opportunity to travel all over England with him. He was also a good companion to be with, an anchor I could lean on, someone I trusted. I was very fond of him but I knew sooner or later I had to go back to Viet Nam and our relationship should have to end. He proposed marriage but I was not in love with him nor was I interested in marriage. My family was my priority. I was very happy and grateful while we were together. Again, life was somehow unpredictable or was it me who unconsciously planned life to turn to my advantage? I very often wondered whether I, in fact, was being manipulative and selfish in order to survive. Thanks to Gia, I could stay in Paris while waiting for the Vietnamese officials to grant me the visa.

One month passed by without any response. I was in an enormous jam. I went to see the Vietnamese Embassy in Paris. I was told that my application had been accepted. They needed to know what branch of the government I wanted to be assigned to, Foreign Affairs or Information. Off the top of my head, I blurted out "Information." Again I was told to wait while they sent my choice back to Viet Nam and awaited the Information Ministry response. The delay could last from one month to several weeks.

Determining to be self-sufficient, I took the risk of looking for a job while I waited. I found that the American Embassy had posted in a French newspaper an opening for a secretary, and applied.

Just coming out of school with no experience whatsoever, I was surprised to receive a letter from the Embassy asking me to come for an interview. At the interview, the officer asked me to type a letter. I looked at the typewriter and as the officer was dictating, I confusedly got up and prepared to leave, I confessed to him that I did not know the keys. The interviewer saw my embarrassment and kindly told me that there were other jobs not requiring typing. By then, I was so ashamed of myself and so shy that I profusely excused myself and slipped out while the poor interviewer stood suspended.

I felt so depressed and hopeless. I had confounded "job interview" with "job offer" and imagined that I was going to start work that day. It only dawned on me when I was told to take dictation that I had to take the test first, and that immediately scared me as I did not know anything at all. I had nobody to help me prepare for the interview or at least to give me advice how to go through an interview.

Much later in life, being more mature and having experience with job interviews, I was convinced that I had let the opportunity slip through my fingers just by a simple misunderstanding. The American official was ready to offer me a job if only I understood the interview technique. I kept rerunning the event in my mind and somehow marveled how my stupidity had turned out to be a blessing. At first I imagined that if I had managed to obtain a job with the Embassy, it would be a bottom line job such as messenger girl or paper-shuffle clerk. How would my life have been? At least, the first order was that I would be able to bring my family to France. I also visualized myself eventually getting married, raising children and contentedly living a peaceful and boring life in France.

Destiny, what else, had reserved me another path for me. "Being stupid or ignorant had its benefits," I congratulated myself when I passed over my past life. I blindly tumbled along; sometimes luck conquered over brain.

Someone above with a magic wand directed me. Innocence had its advantage too; what kind of job could I do at the Ministry of Information?

I chose the Information office because of a silly childhood remembrance.

In 1945, French troops had succeeded in chasing the communists out of power in Viet Nam, re-assuming French authority over the country. For a time, we were refugees in a small village that was in territory the Viet Minh still controlled, to which they had made my father go before my mother discovered where they had banished him and took us there. My father was under house arrest because they had accused him of being pro-French. He was not allowed to go anywhere. French troops were at the door and might overrun the village any day. Finally, the pressure became so great that the Viet Minh made us all flee to the jungle. There, one day, a friend had come to tell him that he had heard the Viet Minh were coming to get both of them that night, and he invited my father to escape with him by boat. My father refused because he was a true nationalist, believing in the independence of the country. It was an enormous mistake. That same night, the Viet Minh came and took my father away.

I vividly remember hearing a racket outside and someone asking the house owner whether my father was here. I heard my mother stirring as she got out of the bed. As we had one room for the whole family to sleep in, I raised my head to watch my mother's movements. She quietly moved to the door and listened to the conversation outside. When she heard the knock, she went to the bed where my father was in deep sleep, loudly snoring. She woke him up and whispered something. He got out of bed wearing shorts and a faded blue undershirt. He opened the door.

"Are you Mr. Tet?" I didn't hear my father's answer. "We come to take you to headquarters."

Then silence returned. I put my face on the pillow and tried to smother my cries. We learned later that his friend did escape by boat that night and arrived safely in Ben Tre, our home town, which we had left when the Viet Minh had banished my father.

My mother tried her best to go on with daily life, taking care of us while, hoping and hoping, she expected my father to return any day. Being too young to be of any help to her, I sensed that she lived in fear and anxiety.

It was one of the most deadly months in the area. Every day, we saw bodies floating on the river behind our rented lodging. My brothers kept watch out for the bodies and ran to alert my mother who immediately followed them to the riverbank, with incense sticks. Each time a body passed by, she stretched out trying to see the face, and gloomily bowed as the body continued its journey downstream.

As summer came to an end, my mother gave up any hope of finding my father alive; she had to return to her job to earn a living and raise her seven young children aged 2 to 10. My mother was told by the proprietor that there was sporadic fighting between the Viet Minh and the French troops on the road, and it was safer for her and the family to walk the 15 kilometers to Ben Tre.

So we got up at 5 a.m. and started our expedition. My youngest 2 year-old brother was put in the traditional basket, with our belongings in another basket. The 15 year-old maid carried both on a wooden pole across her shoulder, balancing our belongings in the basket on one end and my young brother in the one on the other end. My mother held hands with two more of my young brothers while the four oldest children walked behind her.

We took the back roads to avoid troops of both sides. One time on a bridge my mother forced us to crouch down around her while a droning sound was heard in the air. We had no food and no water the whole day. As we reached the outskirts of Ben Tre, my mother decided to go to her colleague's home so we could rest and eat. That was the most nightmarish journey that I and my other siblings ever experienced. We were so exhausted and hungry. But by the time we stopped, we felt so proud of ourselves!

We resumed our normal life under French occupation in Ben Tre. My mother was back teaching and we all went back to school. On several occasions on the way home, I passed by a motorized van with a loudspeaker blasting out propaganda with words that I hardly understood. I collected all the leaflets that they handed out and was very impressed with their flowery narratives about the government and its accomplishments.

Reading was my favorite hobby, thanks to my father. He had always encouraged me to read and somehow it stayed with me. I read anything and everything that fell in my hands, children's books, fairy tales, old newspapers, adult books and even pornography that someone had left around and I picked up to read without understanding the full meaning of it.

So when I encountered so-called "journalists," distributing their leaflets, I was thrilled and admired their talents and speeches. I wanted to be a journalist like them, especially to write and fight against the communists who kidnapped my father and probably tortured and killed him in a cowardly way.

Fragments of childhood memories seemed to linger forever in me. In a small town, civil servants looked so distinguished in a little girl's eyes. I wanted to be prestigious when I grew up. So the words "Information" and "journalists" were imbedded deep in my brain. Strangely, I unconsciously was drawn in that direction without any prevalent consideration.

Now here I was, the French war over with and the country split in two, working in the south, the Republic of Viet Nam, for the Information Ministry. It felt like pre-destination written in my stars.

My first few months with the Department were strange and lonesome. I hardly spoke to anyone, and they seemed to avoid me because of my uniqueness. I was the only woman dressed in Western style in the whole Ministry.

I was aware that being a woman in a patriarchal society, I had to follow a set of protocols and etiquette that I found old fashioned and degrading. I refused to conform. In other words, I defied tradition and challenged the culture by proclaiming my independence. I dressed in Western dresses to go to work while, at the time, Vietnamese women wore the traditional "ao dai."

It was one of the most attractive costumes in Asia and even in the whole world. Ao Dai (literally, "long dress") is a cross between Indian long dress and Chinese traditional dress. The long dress (most often silk of various qualities) is buttoned on one side, and slit on both sides, from the waist to the feet. Underneath the dress, from waist down, a pair of black or white satin loose trousers is worn.

Up until 1975, ao dai was the traditional dress worn daily by all Vietnamese women of all ages and all levels of society. It was colorful and graceful, and sensually wrapped around female bodies, especially young women who seemed to float along the streets. Mme Nhu, who became South Viet Nam's "First Lady", launched a new version of ao dai by getting rid of the high-necked collar and baring the shoulders. It was a daring change that was only appreciated by socialites and young fashionable followers. At the present time, only school girls wear white ao dai, as a school uniform. And women wear them on festive occasions or on wedding day.

Another attractive sight was the way Vietnamese women rode bicycles with their ao dai. They would attach the hind hem to the bicycle's back seat frame so as to keep the dress from being entangled in the back wheel. So along the streets, these sexual bicyclists looked as if they were flying a colorful half-moon shaped silk flap. It was a strange and enchanting sight hat attracted a lot of attention from foreign visitors. Today Saigon (now Ho Chi Minh City) looks like any other big city in the world, the women ndistinguishable from those of any other country, all wearing the same uniform, pantsuits or blue jeans.

I wore Western dress because it was more comfortable and convenient for me in the tropical heat. I wore ao dai for ceremonial days or for special nights out.

At work, I was placed at a desk along with another expatriate, Mary, who had spent many years in Philippines. We exchanged a few polite words although I could see that we had nothing in common. Later I was moved to an enormous square table which occupied the whole room, sharing the table with four clerks, all Southerners.

By now I was very much aware of different accents the people speaking around me had. Most of the high-ranking South Vietnamese officials were originally from the North, among the millions who had fled when the country was partitioned and the communist-controlled north became the Democratic Republic of Viet Nam. In fact I was so disappointed to find very few office workers from the South in our department, except those in lower ranks such as the four clerks with me. Each sat in front of a typewriter. Each day they were given a letter to type, and the rest of the time they were rolling papers into cigarette form, then stringing them together at some length that could be hung on their door. These cigarette-rolls were turned into curtains for their homes, so it was explained to me. I supposed that it might take these women years to complete these curtains.

I wore many hats during my years with the Information Ministry. I was first introduced as translator and interpreter for French and English. That was in the early 1960s, when the country was still peaceful. At first, my boss didn't know what to do with me. Being idle 90% of the time at work, I started bringing novels in to read.

One day my boss found me reading, approached and asked what it was. I showed him the book, one of the fictions of that time.

"Do you like to read?" he asked. He was short, about 55 to 60 years old, a refugee from the North of course, pleasant and charming in a fatherly way.

"Yes, I softly answered.

"Good! Reading is a marvelous hobby," he said, and walked away without further comment.

"Watch it!" whispered the clerk next to me, "he is dangerous." A few minutes later, he came back with a bundle of books. He placed them in front of me and asked me to translate them into Vietnamese. They were English books, and looking closer I realized that they were anti-communist propaganda. My Vietnamese was rusty and more dialect than literary Vietnamese. My friends, the clerks, became my interpreters, translating for me from our Southern dialect into modern Vietnamese so that, I, in turn, could write a more coherent narrative. So day in and day out, I wrote by hand in Vietnamese page after page of anti-communist propaganda. I did finish one book, months later, and brought it to my Minister, who suspiciously glanced at it and pushed it aside.

During the Diem regime, Diem's brother, the notorious and brainy Ngo Dinh Nhu, was the country's second most powerful man. People feared him more than his brother, though. He controlled the youth movement as well as their political party. He decreed that all civil servants, men and women, should wear a blue uniform to go to work, blue Khaki shirt and trousers, not unlike the uniform of our counterparts the communists. We also had to salute the flag every morning prior to work.

I considered the whole thing distasteful and a betrayal of our so-called democratic ideology, copying the communists' image. I intentionally arrived too late at ceremonies. We, the Department of Information in particular, held political meetings once a month in the afternoon. The whole second floor of the building was reserved for these meetings. Mr. T, the second and most dangerous man in the Department, was the speaker. He was easily identified as an ideological cynic, his stern face with thin lips darkened by smoking too many cigarettes, and his darting small eyes sending out threats and casting suspicions. Dressed in blue uniform, he addressed the crowd with punctuated phrases, praising the employees for their loyalty and diving into long tirades on the wickedness and brutality of the Viet Cong.

Against my will, I forlornly followed my colleagues and made myself invisible by sitting in one of the last rows. His speech was lost on me, as I was not too familiar with new Vietnamese diction, and also what I did hear did not interest me. Suddenly I heard my name called. I stood up and was asked to repeat what I had heard from the lecture. I mumbled something.

"Please come up to the micro. We can't hear you." I went up and loudly said that I didn't understand much of what he said. "Miss Le Lieu just came back from France and she still has a lot to learn." The room was silent. I looked straight ahead, profusely blushing, but firmly stayed standing straight. "At least she has the courage to come up to the podium to say so," he smiled sarcastically, and dismissed me. The crowd roared with laughter. I felt completely humiliated and enraged.

"What am I doing in this hole?" I felt sick.

Things turned out much better later. Not knowing what to give me to work, my minister gave me a new title as book censor. It was the happiest time of my life. I read bestsellers from the USA, United Kingdom and other English-speaking countries, and France. Any anti-propaganda books or books mentioning communism instantly would be censored and barred from import. One day I was reprimanded for letting in Webster's Dictionary.

"It's just a dictionary," I said, appalled, wondering whether he was teasing me or simply too ignorant to recognize it as a dictionary.

"I know it's a dictionary, but it has mentioned communism in it." I couldn't believe my ears.

"Are we that moronic?" I asked myself.

"I'll let it go this time but I don't want it to be exhibited in store front windows," he shamelessly persisted. The next day, I passed by a book store, and sure enough the dictionary was not there.

Another day, the minister's wife was sick when he had organized a party for the diplomatic corps. I was asked to help with flowers.

"It's such a simple task, anybody can do it; why me?" I asked, and was confronted by the minister's assistant, who did not say.

I was given money to go to the flower market and buy as many flowers as I wished. I was treated as an important person, being driven in a luxurious French Citroën DS sedan, cars that were officially reserved for dignitaries. I turned my task into a fun game by going from one flower stand to another and buying whatever flowers appealed to me. I was irritated and perplexed at the same time to be asked to do such a simple task. When I got to their house, I set to work arranging the flowers in different vases.

"What are you doing?" I swung around to face a pitiful pale face of a woeful woman. She hardly stayed on her feet while her two arms wrapped around a dressing gown to prevent it from slipping away from her skeleton body.

"Madame, Miss Le Lieu is working on flower arrangements." A male secretary bowed in front of her. She was only in her thirties but was suffering from some kind of illness that decimated her face. She pushed me aside and started cutting the flowers, arranging them gracefully and artfully. I was entranced by her agility and expertise, and exquisite taste. It dawned on me that the minister's wife had taken me for an expert on fashion decoration, considering the way I was dressed. I had never been exposed to any such high society.

Months passed away. I was happy in my little booth with a pile of bestsellers and newly published fiction to pass the time. I became friends with an older woman who had been on this job for years. I recognized her as one of the old guard, educated in French during the French colonial period when French was taught in school more or less as first language.

Tam was in her middle ages with fine features, smartly dressed in ao dai, dignified and nevertheless humble. Her left leg dragged as she walked due to polio or some neural decease that I delicately avoided asking about. We usually spent our lunch together. She was my first friend in that heavily hostile environment.

Being with the Ministry for many years, Tam recognized my frustration and alienation. She filled me in with its politics and its intricate mission. She taught me to be patient and tolerant so as to survive. I enjoyed her company, as we were both from the South. I was overjoyed to have a trusted friend to whom I could openly pour out my worries and anger without any fear.

My first opportunity to use my talent as interpreter happened one day when the Ministry learned that an American journalist would arrive that day. I was taken to the airport to help him through customs. I was informed by the public relations man at the airport that the journalist should be treated with white gloves. I had no idea what to do except to come forward to introduce myself to the stranger and offer him my assistance with customs and passport control.

The American, whose face I still vividly remember, was baffled and suspicious of the whole arrangement. I could see in his eyes fear and defensiveness. Eager to show him our hospitality, I offered to take him downtown in our car, and installed him at the luxurious Majestic Hotel. Once he had signed in, he rudely told me to leave him alone and said he did not need any further assistance. I left with my tail between my legs. Two days later, I received a letter of apology. But from that experience things turned to my favor.

By the end of 1960, Diem and Nhu had tightened their grip, behaving more and more like dictators, terrorizing the people and jailing anyone who spoke ill of their administration. Mme Nhu, Diem's sister-in-law, acted as first lady, lashing out against the foreign press, the American press in particular, and threatening to expel journalists who criticized the regime. She also organized her own "women's movement". The foreign press called her the "Dragon Lady." She intrigued them by her beauty and her outspokenness. At the same time they feared her more than the President. She knew how to use the media to promote herself.

More and more foreign press, mostly American press, came and went almost every week. The conflict between the South and the North started to widen, with Northern support for communist guerrillas, the Viet Cong, in the South. In order to control the foreign press more efficiently, the Saigon government also began to recruit young American-educated Vietnamese for the press service. Some of these new recruits might have worked for the CIA, although there was no evidence to back that up.

During that period, there was a change in the Department of Information. It was no longer a Ministry, as the incumbent minister was promoted to be Minister of Foreign Affairs. In his place, they nominated a director to run the department, and demoted it to be merged into the Ministry of Social Affairs.

The new director, Mr. H., was a medical doctor educated in France and married to a Frenchwoman. Being from the South himself, he took a fancy to me and named me his deputy. From then, things got better for me. With that function, I was his interpreter and in charge of press relations, responsible for calling in the foreign press and helping translate for my boss, who used persuasion and censorship to influence the copy they sent home.

That began my relations with the foreign press, both official and unofficial. As the war started to worsen, more and more foreign journalists arrived. Those were seasonal press whose bases were either in Hong Kong or Singapore or USA and Europe. Most of them came for a few days and then left. I was given responsibility for taking care of foreign correspondents' needs, issuing accreditation cards, and setting up interviews with the President or Mr. or Mme Nhu, or other high-ranking officers. I was also in charge of providing transportation and accompanying the press or the diplomatic corps on various trips outside the city.

I was installed in the office of the Press Club right in the center of the city where most foreign correspondents' offices were located. At last, I was at my place. Journalists dropped by every day either for my service or just to chat, hoping to get some accidental information out of me. My star was rising, I entertained and was entertained. I met new faces, and old friends who came back when there was big (bad) news to cover. I was so efficient and appreciated by the foreign press that words of praise began to reach my superiors. One day, I was told by my boss that President Diem was interested in meeting me.

That day I was driven to the Presidential Palace. My boss received me at the entrance and hustled me into a huge, spacious but somehow empty, reception room and asked to wait there on a huge couch in a corner. I trembled with fear, tongue-tied. I had never had any desire to meet that man, whose path I had crossed several times during trips with his diplomatic guests visiting newly-created immigrant centers or a battle field just victoriously re-taken by the government army. During these trips, I just stayed in the shadows, being told that Diem hated women.

I did not know what form of meeting awaited me, formal or ceremonial? I was a nobody, unless I had betrayed some indiscretion or some state secret. I sat there and felt the icy calmness around me. Suddenly, I heard some rustle in a far corner and looked up to see another Ngo, the Archbishop, Diem's brother, and most revered Head of the Catholic Church in Saigon. He stopped at the staircase and turned to look at me a minute in silence and went on. I sat still. Suddenly a flash went through my mind. He might expect me to stand up to bow or to kneel down as his subject, begging for his benediction. I was not Catholic and not religious. I just sat there staring back at him, a bit thrilled at first, contemptuous later for what he represented.

Within five minutes, Mr. H. came to lead me to the adjacent room. As I entered, I felt a chill, the room was small and in semi-darkness and Diem was standing in the middle, facing me with knitted eyebrows, in his usual white suit, arms akimbo showing his rotund belly. I bowed my head.

"Mr. President, this is Miss Le Lieu from the Information bureau. The foreign press appreciated her performance and praised her for her good work." Mr. H's voice trailed off, or I was too confused to hear the rest.

Diem mumbled some inaudible words and shook my hands and walked away. I was ushered out of the door without further words. That was my reward for rendering good service to the country.

"What a joke!" I smiled at Mr. H, who had been in a cowardly rush to get back to his office. I went back to my office and resumed my duties, satisfied to have friends around.

Then Malcolm showed up in my office, one week after I had seen him in the street. And my life changed forever.

CHAPTER TWO

Thinking again about my first glimpse of Malcolm walking down Pasteur Street and saying I thought he would ask me for a date, I was simply making a sarcastic remark and teasing myself. In reality, I knew that one way or the other he would have to see me for accreditation. So I continued home, carefree and looking forward to a relaxing evening.

My house was neither luxurious nor in a so-called upper class neighborhood. Its location was inadvertently situated between the rich and elite class and the commercial area. I was attracted by its charm and tranquility. Later when I learned more through my frequent trips around town, I realized that our home was actually in the most desirable location.

The cottage was hidden behind the big and busiest boulevard in Saigon that stretched from the central market to the outskirts. Boulevard Pasteur, named after the French scientist, was known for its wideness and the many famous landmarks lining its shady length. These included the Gia-Long Palace, the former Emperor Bao Dai's residence whenever he came to the South, now reserved for foreign dignitaries visiting Viet Nam. There was a stretch of big boa trees, flamboyant trees and other exotic trees and flowers that were displayed in the middle of the boulevard and in front of the Palace. The Catholic Cathedral and its spacious plaza was one block from the Palace. Many government ministries including mine were also located along Pasteur Boulevard. Interwoven between these official colonial-style two-storied buildings stood several privately owned villas hidden behind impeccably landscaped flower gardens. Their owners belonged to the privileged class or resided in various embassies. As on most streets in Saigon, huge tamarind trees with hanging fruit were intermixed with beautiful flamboyant trees, known for their flaming red flowers, all helping to preserve the elegance and grace of past French influence. The Pearl of Orient, Saigon was called, no exaggeration at that time.

During the dry season and when it was not too hot, I enjoyed walking home along the boulevard, enjoying the coolness of the sunset and dreaming of living in one of those marvelous and cozy villas. Being new to the city and unfamiliar with the environment, I thought the cottage was a haven for me and a boost for my ego and self-respect.

Again I was so lucky to find such a hideout in such a desirable area.

Also, though this was unplanned, my cottage was on the same street as my office and the Associated Press office. Daily, after work, I hailed a cyclo which took me directly to my home, passing by the Associated Press, where Malcolm also lived. Was this another coincidence?

I had chosen to work in the Information office because of some silly childhood remembrance. It had something to do with the war and the disappearance of my father, to me the dearest and most beloved member of my family. Being deprived of his love, I strongly felt as if I were on a boat with no steering, floating along, pumping, then breaking up and hoping for the best and the goodness of any soul who would give me a hand before I sank. Having no one close to me to give me advice or guidance, I mostly acted by impulse or at random.

To explain my impulse to choose the Information office, I had to go back, way back when I was still a little girl, during World War II, the Japanese war in Asia. I was about 9 years old. We lived in Ben Tre, a town of some 100,000 or less that was famous for being a communist stronghold and for its pretty girls. It is situated in the flat and fertile Mekong River Delta, about 50 miles south of Saigon. My father was the second man, under his French boss, in the department of Land Development. We lived in a two-story house attached to another identical house, the pair standing alone between a Chinese school on one side and a row of Jewelry stores on the other side. Two brilliant flamboyant trees flanked the two houses. My mother was a teacher at the primary school where all of us went through our childhood. Our neighbors were business people, jewelers, and the Chinese school.

My father used to take us to watch basketball games at the Chinese school. We were not allowed to enter the premises, so my father would lift us up to sit on the concrete wall surrounding the school.

Ben Tre was considered a big town in the Delta. To go to or from Saigon, we would take a "location" [French for "hire"], a private bus that ran from the town to the ferry, along rice fields and coconut groves and scattered farmers' houses. It was the most beautiful and exotic scenery, which unfortunately has slowly disappeared in our time. Approaching the entrance to Ben Tre, there was a roundabout plaza with an obelisk in its center, with the public stadium on one side and well-kept villas on the other.

One then went into town along a tree shaded route, passing government villas, boys' and girls' separate schools, a pagoda with the smell of incense floating in the air and the sound of occasional gong bells striking. Then the central market in the middle of town on the way to the river. Two-storied shops lined the market, most of them owned by Chinese.

During the market days, the river was busy with buying and selling both on land and on the river boats. My mother used to take me to buy live fish on a houseboat where merchants and their families lived. I always wished that we could have a home on the river ourselves. It would be romantic and charming.

My parents used to take us for walks during weekends along the river, so wide that crossing on a ferry was an adventure in itself. Along the river there were benches to sit on, shaded by big boa, flamboyant, and tamarind trees, and even weeping willows. On the other side of the road stood beautiful official villas and the Province Chief's Palace, a modest French style mansion.

Occasionally, my parents took us to visit friends on the other side of the river. I was told that only the not-well-to-do or peasants lived there. I was enchanted by the groves of coconut trees laden with coconuts that lined the back road. My parents' friends always fed us with fresh coconut juice, pieces of sugar cane or corn powder. Pigs, chicken, dogs and cats roamed freely in the dirt.

Other weekends, we went out of town by bicycle for picnics. My father first taught me how to ride, with a three-wheel bike. And once I managed on a two-wheel bike, he always rode by my side to keep an eye on me. When I was too exhausted and no longer able to pedal, he would reach out and hold my arm, pushing me along as we rode on to the picnic site. I supposed that my sister was still too young to participate in these expeditions.

Our family had moved to Ben Tre from Tra Vinh, another town in the Mekong Delta where I and my five siblings were born, except for the youngest. My mother's family lived in Tra Vinh, and we had many occasions to go back to visit them. We used to take a ferry, which took almost the whole day.

One day while we were in school, we heard a big explosion as if a bomb had gone off in our neighborhood. Within an hour we learned that the Tra Vinh ferry had exploded because of a gas leak. A colleague and friend of my mother's perished with it, along with her children, and that was the end of the ferry service.

I could go on describing my childhood. The more I wrote the more nostalgic I became. It was the happiest time of my life. And I believed that my parents represented a perfect family couple.

I went back in 1994 with Malcolm to Ben Tre. I could not find the street where we lived, and our house no longer existed. The bustling market had extended beyond it and turned the neighborhood into a shambles of dirt and people, thousands of people.

Ben Tre had changed hands not once but several times during my life. The first one was under the French colonial period in 1943, when the Japanese invaded Vietnam and took over. But that time was the end of our peaceful and happy life.

Being too young then to understand fully all the suffering that my parents went through during the fall of French domination and the invasion of Japanese troops in our town, I can remember only fragments of events that touched my family during that period.

My parents used to travel within Viet Nam, anywhere from Hanoi to the central mountains every summer vacation. I saw pictures of my two eldest brothers on the famous lake in Hanoi, or my sister and me riding on a horse in Dalat, a famous mountain resort. Suddenly, one summer vacation before the war broke out, the family apparently had financial difficulties and our parents could not afford to bring all of us with them. They announced that only one of us could accompany them. That year was my turn. Our vacation was in Cambodia. I remember the hotel room on the edge of the Angkor Wat temples. It had a very imperial baldaquin on top of the bed, with mosquito-netting neatly tucked with a colorful ribbon, undone at night to surround the whole bed.

The hotel had a wide balcony where I spent a lot of time looking with fear at the thick dark forest facing our hotel, expecting some kind of monster to burst out at any moment. I remember we went into the forest once and a dark man approached my father, showing him a dagger. My father bought it, against my mother's wishes. She mumbled something like the man might be an assassin and my father shouldn't have talked to him. She sighed with relief when he got the dagger and teased her, brandishing it in front of her.

I was afraid of taking a walk in that dark forest and being pursued by screaming monkeys on the trees. We reached the famous Angkor Wat, built in the 13th Century with long stone walls with relief carvings, and wide staircases carved with monsters and snakes. In the eyes of a young child, it was a nightmarish experience and I could not wait to get away. I vaguely listened to my father's explanation of the history of the place.

(I returned there in 1972 with Malcolm, but only to stand in the distance to observe the gate. Dark figures were dashing around behind it. The temples were then occupied by the Khmer Rouge, who could take us under fire. For me, it was a sad sight for me.)

On the way back from Cambodia, my parents took a boat, on which there were Japanese soldiers lying around along the rail. My father struck up a conversation with two or three of them during the voyage and even shared lunch with them. I believed that they communicated with him in French.

I also remembered that one day we saw a group of Japanese soldiers camping behind our school. Once school let out, a friend of mine took me to the gate separating the Japanese military compound from our school. We just waved at them and giggled when they came and gave us candies. When I told my mother of the encounter, I was reprimanded and forbidden to do it again. Then one day, the Japanese vanished. The reason didn't register on me then, accepting their presence and their disappearance as normal.

One morning, I woke up because a great tumult of thousands of Vietnamese black-clad men passing in front of our house, yelling and singing. My father told us that our country was now free and independent, with Ho Chi Minh as President. Between the departure of the Japanese and the reappearance of French forces, he had proclaimed independence.

For me, it didn't mean much. My father had to go for training early in the morning before going to work. I saw him tuck the dagger that he bought in the forest into the side of his trousers. (My mother told us much later that she had buried it behind our house in Ben Tre.) In my eyes, my father was my hero.

One morning, I woke up and was told that my father had been arrested in the night. My mother had gone to visit her family in Tra Vinh. Later I picked up from conversations between my mother and my grandmother that the Viet Minh had accused my father of being pro-French and therefore a traitor.

The name Ho Chi Minh came up in school and we, young school girls, had to salute the flag and his picture every morning. It was a puzzle for me because a few months before, we had been taught to salute and sing in French lauding Maréchal Pétain, the Vichy French leader ("Maréchal, Maréchal, nous voilà,"etc…), whose picture hung in every classroom.

And then overnight we had been told to sing a new Vietnamese anthem, the tune and some lyrics of which I still remember. It was a very patriotic and powerful tune, something like "Viet Nam beloved, Viet Nam the victor…" So every time my brothers and I would catch a fish, we would joyously sing out "mackerel flies" to the anthem tune.

One day, my sister and I were singing another very popular and nationalist song, "Once we leave, we'd never return," and my father snapped at us to stop, saying "There is no such thing to leave and never come back." We both were puzzled to see such an emotional reaction from my father for such a song, although we did not clearly grasp its meaning. We never sang it.

I was 9 years old when l lost my father. I have missed him all these decades even now that I am 82, I still long to be able to call him father and to snuggle against him. In a way, I still feel I am his little girl. I have often wondered whether my other siblings have felt the same way. I don't believe that my twin brothers did. They were 16 months older than I and died several years ago. They suffered under my father's terrible temper when he taught them at home. He shouted at them and often slapped my brothers very hard on the face when they didn't know the subject or couldn't do the calculation. My brothers were terrified of him. My mother either tried to stop him or wept in silence.

I remember my father as a tall man, good looking with a round kind face, and a bit overweight. He was the one to teach me anything that a little girl growing up had to learn. He was passionate about Chinese chess, and often forgot his own meals to keep playing. He taught me to play with him and if by accident, I beat him, he'd take me in his arms and place a kiss on my cheek. One year near the end of his life, he hired a judo teacher to give my twin brothers and me lessons. Early in the morning, we were in our back yard, kicking and waving our hands. I was included in all activities that my twin brothers did. I was more or less a tomboy.

My father often played tennis after work. He also loved to cook fried noodles at weekends for the family. I loved him dearly and was also terrified when he became angry. According to my mother, I was his favorite. He bought children's books for me to read and he took me to soccer games. He surprised me one day when with a bunch of a dozen sugar canes because I had expressed my fondness of cracking them and sucking all that sweet juice out until there was nothing left but dried fibers. I could talk to him and be more relaxed with him than with my mother. In my young mind, parents loved all children and nobody was a particular favorite; at least, I was not aware of being his favorite, though I suspected that my sister might be my parents' favorite because she was younger and cuter.

I was never really close to my mother. At first, when my father disappeared, I started to assume some responsibilities such as taking care of my younger brothers and doing some housework. My twin brothers were never home after school. They seemed to be free of all responsibilities and liberated from my father's authority. Home was for them to come back to sleep and to eat. My mother had no control over them or any other boy after them. On the other hand, my mother continued to love my twin brothers more than any of us. Any crises they encountered, my mother went out of her way to defend them even after they were adults and had their own families.

During this time of Viet Minh rule before the French returned, there were constant rumors of public executions in the town stadium. One day, after class, my classmates rushed out dragging me with them to the stadium which was located some ten minutes' walk from our school. A big crowd blocked the entrance and we struggled to climb up the stadium stairs. We were forbidden to get in. By then I learned that five men were about to be executed, and I returned home disappointed not to have seen it. As soon I stepped into the house, I saw people gathered around a couch where my mother was lying and crying. I was told that my mother had had a fit because she thought that my father was one of the victims.

In 1945, French troops began chasing the Vietnamese communists out of power and re-assuming authority and control over the country. Fighting took place in the North and near Saigon, but the Viet Minh continued their control in the Delta. My father was neither freed nor heard of. It was during the summer vacation of that year that mother decided to go and search for him.

Every day, she left the house early, accompanied by Manh, a good man who worked as an aide to our neighbor, the owner of a bicycle shop in front of our house. She came back exhausted and disappointed at not finding my father. But one day she came home at around 5 p.m. and told us we were packing immediately to go to Cai Quao, a small village some 15 kilometers from Ben Tre. She had hired a boat and we rushed to load our mattresses and all household items on it.

Overloaded, the boat slowly left that night. I was in heaven, not only imagining that very soon I would see my father again, but also to be near water. I lay on a pile of mattresses in the middle of the boat. The sky was pitch black and dotted with trillions of stars. From time to time I saw a dart of light in the sky. I was too young to recognize it as a meteorite. But I was so enchanted by the beauty of the sky and the regular sounds of the oars slapping on the water as the boat silently slid along. I was alone outside, breathing in all the sights and sounds along the Mekong River. I was in heaven. I didn't realize that the boat owner and my mother were both scared that it could sink at any moment if it was rocked by another passing boat.

In the morning, I saw we were approaching a house on the riverbank. And my father's silhouette appeared. "Could it be that our house is right on the water?" I jumped up with joy.

My father looked good and had not changed a bit. He was overjoyed to see us all and we ran to inspect our new home, where the Viet Minh had sent him and put him under house arrest. It turned out that it was more a wooden hut than a house. The floor was made of patted mud and it consisted of a small living room of which a double wooden bed was placed in a front corner and another bigger wooden bed at the back and in between a small dining table. The roof was made of dried coconut branches, a normal construction of all peasants' houses in rural areas. A small coconut branched roof attached to the side of the hut and on the edge of the river was our kitchen. The community outhouse was crude, made of coconut branches as walls and the toilet seat consisted of two wide wooden boards. Below the seat was the river. There were two outhouses shared by the neighborhood. For us, children, anything new was exciting and challenging. For me, all I cared was to be with my father again and living at the edge of the river.

At that time, we were refugees among the communists. For a few months we led a peaceful life, fishing, swimming. My younger siblings went to school and my father had to go to report to the Viet Minh office once every week. In the evening, my parents took us for a walk in a dirt road behind the school. When it rained, the road was slippery and full of pot holes where fish took refuge during floods..

I learned to swim for the first time under my father's supervision. Time passed for many months or many weeks, I couldn't tell.

One day, our parents told us to pack up and we moved to another place.

French troops were at the door and might overrun the village any day. The Viet Minh officials ordered my father to move farther inside the country. Somehow we ended up sharing a house, with its peasant owner, in the jungle. It was there that I had experienced a memorable scene of a so-called "harvest festival," that I had read about in Vietnamese romantic fictions in school.

One moving experience for me was that I actually had an opportunity to witness a true ceremonial harvest day, not just through books and Vietnamese plays or movies. I had often conjured up in my mind how romantic it would be to be able to participate in such an event – the celebration of the end of hard-working months in rice fields and the beginning of gathering fruit and long repose.

That dreamlike visual of peasants' life provoked a strong emotion in me, romantic, simplistic, innocent and outright magical; but I never imagined I would have an opportunity to be in it. The harvest season fell in the month of September when the monsoon season was over. Peasants would begin to cut the rice stalks and sell them to the landlord. On a certain day fixed by looking at the moon and the celestial calendar, the community, made up of everal families, got together and stacked the harvest rice stalks in a circle on he concrete commune yard, as large as a rice field. They then set two cows n top of the pile and led them marching round and round the hay, a way of eparating the rice grains from the stalks, which usually took the whole night. When it became dark, food and wine were served. It was also a fun time for he families to relax.

Young Vietnamese men drank and sang love songs that they impro- ised on the spot to flirt with young village girls. In Vietnamese it was called 'ho". I had heard these songs on the radio and in Vietnamese literature and hey evoked strong imagination and emotions in me. Now it truly happened as lescribed in books that I had read. I was so thrilled by the show. Unfortunately, t was at the darkest time for my parents.

After my father was taken away forever by the Viet Minh, as I recount- d in the previous chapter, we returned home to Ben Tre. We all felt like en- ering a tomb. It was desolate and empty, and my mother almost fainted with grief while we, the children, quietly unloaded and prepared to bed. The pres- nce of our father seemed so strong and I missed him so much that tears were unning down my cheeks in silence.

We resumed our normal life, now again under French occupation.

But the house next door was requisitioned and turned into a torture hamber.

Despite the thick wall separating the two houses, we could hear screams f pain day and night. During week-ends, whenever my mother saw a uni- ormed officer coming up the street towards our house, my mother gathered ll of us and took us to the market. We often rode our bicycle, making several ours around the market place while my mother sat near a column where she ould watch the house. As soon as she saw the black car pull away, she called is back to head home.

My mother continued to teach and we went to school. Often when chool let out and I walked home, I crossed a group of men who introduced hemselves as journalists from the Information Office. So when I encountered hese so called "journalists," who distributed propaganda leaflets in the streets, thought they were patriotic. I was thrilled and envied their positions. I told nyself that when I grew up, I wanted to be a "journalist" like them. I wanted o write and fight against the communists who had kidnapped my father, prob- ıbly tortured him and killed him like cowards.

In a small town, through a little girl's eyes, these civil servants looked so listinguished. The words "information," "propaganda" and "journalists" were embedded deep in my brain. Now, many years later, here I was, working for the Ministry of Information.

One week after I saw Malcolm in the street, he showed up in my office

"Here he is," I smiled to myself. He wore a long sleeved white shirt, and the khaki trousers, the same clothes I had seen him wearing in the street.

"Are you Miss Le Lieu?" he looked serious and insecure. He introduced himself and took out his passport and the letter of introduction from the Associated Press.

"I have heard a lot about you from John Griffin. I am honored to meet you." We shook hands and I invited him to sit down while I processed his papers of accreditation.

"I also have two wishes to ask for a favor," he smiled.

"Yes, how can I help?" I could guess.

"I would like to interview Mme Nhu," I took note.

"I heard that there would be a military operation in the Delta sometime this week. I would like permission to participate in that operation." He took a puff on his cigarette.

"I can't promise you at this time; I have to submit your request through the Defense Department," I said, and calmly warned him not to expect a lot. "I will do my best and will call you later." He got up and politely clapped his two hands in the manner of greeting and bowed. I clumsily folded my hands in response. He turned to go and then swung back, looking me in the eye.

"Would you like to have dinner with me some evening?" I smiled.

"Sure," I politely answered without conviction. Malcolm bowed once more and left.

Mother, Nguyen thi Le, left, with her sister.

Father, Huynh van Tet, as a young man.

My parents, right, with my eldest twin brothers and my mother's niece and her husband in Hanoi, in 1938.

My twin brothers, my sister and me on horseback in Dalat, around 1939.

My mother, sitting, with the seven children and a niece, around 1946. I am sitting on the extreme right and my cousin is standing in the middle.

CHAPTER THREE

I took Malcolm's invitation in stride. I had been going out for dinner and dancing with foreign journalists and members of the diplomatic corps who were interested in my company and had felt more comfortable with some than with others.

For the first six months since I was back, I had spent every evening alone at home after work. My two student brothers came home for dinner and went out with friends until past nighttime. On some special occasions my sister's husband, Philippe, would take us out to a French restaurant or night clubs. Otherwise, I spent my evenings cooking meals for the next day. I had been invited by Vietnamese acquaintances or military officers whom I encountered while accompanying President Diem's trips to military bases. I was not very enthusiastic or interested in them because I never felt comfortable in their company. I began to wonder whether I was going to spend the rest of my life as a spinster.

Once more, fate intervened. One day my Minister asked me to attend a gala that the Ministry had organized to welcome a group of newly-arrived foreign journalists in the famous Hotel Continental, the most luxurious and prestigious French hotel. It was located at a corner of Catinat Street, the Fifth Avenue of Saigon, and Boulevard Bonnard, another elegant and wide avenue.

The hotel was built at the beginning of the 20th Century in a French style, a three- storied brick mansion with high-ceiling rooms and a wide sidewalk terrace. The Continental had been exclusively for French and Western guests during the French occupation, and only on rare occasions visited by Vietnamese dignitaries.

During my childhood, the hotel was the symbol of luxury and class frequented only by the French colonial masters and their families. It was a time when segregation was pronounced. French was forced upon us as first language in all schools. And yet, socially we (the "Annamites", so the French called us at that time) were inferior to their class. The first time that I met a French man face to face was when a friend of my mother paid a surprising visit to our house.

I still remember the surprising effect on all of us when one evening, as we young children were getting ready for bed, we saw a mixed couple dropping in with their luggage.

The woman was small, less than 5ft tall, about my mother's age, (I was too young to guess,) and skinny, with short wavy hair, a new fashionable style for Ben Tre. She wore the traditional ao dai. Her husband was French, very tall, handsome and looked younger than she. He and my father shook hands and exchanged greetings in French. My mother was excited, fussing around the couple. Mme Su was my mother's classmate and friend. She and her husband happened to be passing through Ben Tre on their way back to Saigon.

I and my siblings gathered on the steps of the ladder. We were speechless and thrilled to have a white man in the house. In no time, words got around and our door was blocked with young kids in the neighborhood. They were like us, at first frozen with awe, then they got bolder, chattering and laughing and gesturing in the stranger's direction. My father chased them away and closed the door.

We were ushered upstairs to our beds. It was a rare sight to receive a mixed couple in our house. Mixed couples, mostly a Vietnamese woman married to a French man, were and still are regarded as unacceptable in Vietnamese society. Later on, I was the victim of racial bias myself. I also reflected in the aftermath that my father's being marked as pro-French ultimately resulted in his arrest and murder.

The Continental Hotel in Saigon was popular with foreigners because it was right in the center of everything. It still stands, on one side of the old handsome whitewashed Opera House that was built during the French colonial time. Diem turned it into the Parliament, and that it remained until the Communist regime after 1975 returned it to its original use. It still is the Opera House today.

Givral, a café/restaurant, and also the foreign press's favorite gathering place, was opposite the Continental. Rows of two-storied buildings lodged expensive department stores, an international book store, a café and several restaurants along Catinat and Bonnard streets. These streets with French names were changed to Vietnamese names during Diem's regime. But members of the old guard like me and others of my generation preferred or unconsciously continued to use their French names.

There were two other luxurious hotels in Saigon at that time -- the "Majestic", another French-style hotel along the Saigon River at the end of Catinat Street, and the Caravelle, opposite the Continental on the other side of the Opera, a modern eight-story "skyscraper" that was the tallest building in Saigon. Most of American press made their offices and living quarters there. The Caravelle offered air-conditioned rooms and an outdoor restaurant/night club on the rooftop. The foreign press used it after Diem as an observation post during the frequent coups d'État and counter-coups that followed.

The Continental was for the Europeans who preferred old-fashioned luxury and were nostalgic. The hotel decoration was simple but elegant with French imported chandeliers: ceiling fans constantly and slowly whirled around to lower the heat and at the same time, to caress the idea of life in slow and sensual motion.

Three or four steps led guests from the lobby to a spacious restaurant furnished with small dark mahogany round tables and deep leather black-cushioned round-shaped arm chairs similar to those in European private clubs. High accordion- folded ceiling-to-floor glass windows opened out to a wide and elevated terrace, where guests could relax and watch pedestrians and beautiful women passing by while sipping Pernot or some other aperitif.

The terrace area was surrounded by enormous terracotta containers on which tall fuchsia bushes served to deaden the noise outside and provide privacy and shade. The pale purple flowers softened the glaring tropical sunlight during the day and perfumed the surrounding area at night.

I had never had occasion to be inside the Continental rooms, but I was told by the regulars that they were spacious with large French windows and high ceiling fans. It was there that spies, dissidents, political plotters and warmongers were drawn. The movie "Ugly American," written by Graham Greene, was filmed at this very hotel.

As soon as the sun set and the city lights started to glitter in the streets, and the heat was blown away by gentle caressing breezes, the Continental terrace turned into a lively place. All tables inside and outside were, in no time, filled with regulars or newly arrived guests. Foreigners, in addition to well-off Vietnamese in ties and jackets, sipped drinks with friends, exchanged business with partners or else idly debated politics among themselves.

I often thought back to these nostalgic evenings, of sinking into a soft leather-cushioned wicker arm-chair and being lulled by the soft French music in the soft light on the terrace, feeling transported to another world, magical and elusive.

Saigon, that "Pearl of the Orient," had that mystical effect on everybody. It provided some kind of false peace and comfort. I myself was part of that experience. And for foreign journalists, the city in the evening was surreal, troublesome and pulsating with pretty girls, good food and excitement. For these journalists, where was the reality? War, mangled bodies, bombs and cries of agony and despair during the day suddenly dissipated in the breezy sunset as they savored exotic Vietnamese dishes and flirted with their girlfriends. They couldn't believe that they had witnessed all the horrors of war a few hours ago risking their lives and being shot at and had come back to the city, changed into ties and well-pressed jackets. The Continental terrace atmosphere was like that, surreal and unnatural.

My first introduction to that society happened with the gala given by the Ministry of Information that evening when I was personally asked to attend.

Eager to improve the government's relationship with the foreign press, the Ministry was willing to shell out money to impress them with its hospitality, including drinks, fancy delicacies and even an orchestra. The minister asked me to serve as hostess/interpreter. I was flattered but nervous at the beginning to see so many foreigners and foreign dignitaries in that vast area. As the band started, I suddenly found myself surrounded by journalists, most of them Americans, inviting me to dance. I loved dancing and in no time I was the belle of the evening. At the end of the evening, I was offered a ride home and a date.

After that, I got bolder and ventured out on dates. "Dates," to my understanding at that time, meant going out to have dinner and fun with a friend. Most of the journalists were married and came for one or two weeks to cover some political crisis such as a Viet Cong attack, a coup d'État, or an bomb that had detonated in some restaurant and killed American soldiers.

I had never met any American, civilian or military, before I returned home to Vietnam from Europe, so I did not fully understand their culture and habits. I was shocked and offended by their frank talk and obnoxious remarks, and I did not see the humor in their jokes.

The "United States" as a country had never entered my vocabulary before. To me "United States" was a far-away land depicted in some fairy tale or in movies. Even when I lived in Europe, American tourists, both men and women, were looked upon as a bunch of giants, with a lot of money to throw away. They represented wealth, fancy cars, and for me, they were extraterrestrial, because they didn't look like anybody else and spoke an alien language. They were recognized by their clothing, their physiology and their loud mouths.

Later, after Malcolm and I were married, we went back to New York City, his hometown, and I kept asking myself where were all these tall Americans I had seen overseas. The New York women in the streets looked very much like any ordinary women in Europe. On the other hand, I was not disillusioned about American men like those I met in Vietnam. They were tall and incredibly affable.

The first thing that drew me to them was their manner towards women. They exhibited a gallantry I never experienced before - helping me to cross the street, pulling out the chair for me to sit down or get up. They were courteous and solicitous. In other words, I was treated as an important person. I lived in Paris for several years. French men were famous for being gallant, but they paled next to the American men. Being transported by such splendid customs, I sometimes forgot that this group of journalists in Saigon was a special species.

Some of them were liars and deceivers, in a city that was full of them. I had been duped, used, insulted and deceived by some ambitious, nutty journalists who sometimes behaved much like imperialists, trying to use me to extract some information or confirmation of political rumors, or simply interesting gossip that would help them write their stories.

Others were lonely, missing their family and did not want to spend dinner by themselves. They were always correct and decent. I, on the other hand, had nothing to lose, because I had no political secrets and was not interested in meddling with politics. I was an alien in my own country and I connected better with foreigners than my own people.

Ironically, I had learned a lot from these journalists. They lost their tongues when they got drunk or when they felt upset by the events of the day. They had to have someone to whom to spill out their guts. I was part of their euphoria.

I was, in no way, an angel. Nor was I a drifter, although sometimes I felt like a broken branch drifting along with the flow, letting destiny take charge. I had no one close enough to share my thoughts with. My mother was in Ben Tre and had her own problems with her school master. Being a widow at the age of 40, she had to fight for survival in a male- dominated school. Every time she brought a man back to the house, she not only faced critical looks from her neighbors, but also anger from us children. We were too young to understand her loneliness, but suspicious of anybody taking our father's place. I suspected that she secretly hid her love affairs from us.

"You were all mean to me," my mother said one day as I happened to be alone with her. "I don't understand why you are still obsessed by what I did." I felt some reproach and bitterness in her tone. "I am just curious, that's all," I shyly told her, lowering my voice. "I am sorry if I offended you." I never touched the subject again.

My twin eldest brothers were never interested in the family. Being liberated from our father's grips, they were most of the time absent from home. They disappeared from the time they woke up to the time they came home for dinner and bedtime. They had no male adult to teach them discipline and responsibility. The one brother who seemed more homebound and serious became alcoholic and lost his life on the road, leaving four young children behind. My sister and I, (with credit to my sister during my ten years of absence) were left to hold on to family traditions and to assume the financial burden of schooling for our youngest brothers.

Very often I longed to have a male friend whom I could trust to support me in my moments of doubts and distress. Growing up far away from the family, I looked for some male friend who might love me enough to stand by my side, a father figure or at least a caring brother. Many of my girlfriends would have laughed at my naivety.

"It doesn't exist in life," they mocked me.

"Why not?" I insisted. "Men are also capable of being loyal friends without any other intentions."

"Yes, have you found one?" Yes and no, I could always count on someone for help in heavy jobs or difficult tasks that I could not handle. But they were never around to lend a shoulder for me to lean on when I was in distress.

Now, I had an interesting job, socializing with the elites, both high-ranking Vietnamese military and politicians, and the foreign press. But the country was at war. The government was corrupted and unstable. Being in the middle of such turmoil I was always in the state of fear and insecure. I was in the middle of a mental crisis.

I was young, at an age that the French singer Édith Piaf called "La vie en rose." I was vain, ambitious, selfish and full of energy and optimism. I wanted to enjoy myself while opportunities offered. There was no harm in dating, I argued with myself. I was aware of the moral codes inflicted on Vietnamese women. Girls and women could not go out with men unless they were engaged to be married. And we were not supposed to go out with foreigners. We wanted to preserve our pure race. We regarded foreigners as outsiders who did not respect us and who were only interested in sex. So whoever went out with them was labeled as prostitute or bar-girl.

"Your people are more racists than we are," Malcolm used to comment. Walking with a foreigner, I was chased by children, mocking and insulting me while street vendors and passers-by echoed their shouts. After our marriage, one day, we were in a taxi and Malcolm got out to deliver a letter to a friend, and I remained in the car waiting for him. Suddenly, the taxi driver whispered: "How long have you been sleeping with him?" I was so stunned that it took me a minute to react.

"What did you say?" I yelled out. Ever since, we took separate taxi to go to parties or dinners in town.

I was repeatedly told since I was a child that grown-up girls' place was at home. I despised Confucius' teachings. I was lucky to have a modern mother who worked outside the home. "You have to be independent as a woman." She single- handedly sent me and my sister to the prestigious French schools in Saigon, and later sent me to Paris.

"Don't believe in anything taught by Confucius. I even dislike him myself." That was my mother. My mother never objected to my going out with foreigners. She had a soft side for the French, on the whole. She was never shy about praising anything related to them or their culture. Her mortal enemies despised her for that and used it as a reason to accuse my father of being pro-French. When my mother came to stay with us in Saigon, I told her my experiences with my dates. She enjoyed hearing me describing such and such a journalist. My dates kept me entertained at least once or twice a week. Most of the time they were new ones, as new journalists arrived. I dined in the most expensive restaurants offering rich international culinary delights from Vietnamese to Chinese, French, Spanish, Scandinavian, and Moroccan.

Soon the unexpected happened, without any warning. One day in the office, I received J.R., a new arrival, a freelance journalist for Time Magazine. He asked permission to cover the Vietnamese Air Force on an ongoing operation in the Delta. I had no time to write down his request to my minister before I was interrupted by the arrival of an NBC team led by the producer Fred R.

"I hear that there is an ongoing military operation today. I and my team want to be there," Fred loudly told me without any formal introduction. "Can I see your boss?"

"Please wait here. I go and see if the minister is free." I got up and went into the Minister's office.

Fred barged in behind me. "Excuse me Minister, I am Fred R., NBC producer. NBC is making a documentary film on Vietnam along with the famous actor Ralph Bellamy as narrator." Fred loudly spewed out a rapid tirade about the film they were going to make.

My boss and I were at a loss. I was not so sure I understood the whole thing, while my boss scowled at me. But when he heard Ralph Bellamy was in town, he cheerfully dispatched me to accompany them to the airport. Meanwhile, J. R. was still patiently waiting in my office. I signaled for him to follow me. I arranged to requisition a government car to take me and J.R. to the airport. The NBC team already had arranged their own transportation.

Out in the street, as we were waiting for the car, Fred took my arm and dragged me to his car while J.R. was gazing at me bewildered. As the car sped away, I anxiously looked back to make sure that he was given the government car so he could follow. J.R., silhouetted standing on the sidewalk, continued to keep his eyes on our car. I felt angry for being badly treated. J.R. finally caught up with us at the airport and I embarked all of them on a fighter aircraft we found waiting on the runway.

The next day, I received a phone call from Fred apologizing for his behavior and inviting me to attend a dinner given by his Vietnamese associate in Ralph Bellamy's honor. I had never heard of the actor before although I thought I knew all the famous American actors at that time. I was flattered and looked forward to meeting one in the flesh.

He was a disappointment. He looked like any ordinary middle aged American man, with undistinguished features, downturned eyelids, thin lips and brownish skin. He had the stature of a cross between John Wayne and Fredric March. He was composed and chain-smoked. I was a movie buff and knew almost all male American actors. But I had never seen, nor heard of Ralph Bellamy. I was enlightened many years later when I lived abroad.

The dinner at the Vietnamese associate's turned out to be a small party consisting of Bellamy, Fred and me. The hostess laid out an elaborate Vietnamese meal that was tasty and better than any restaurant's. I was seated next to Fred. He directed the conversation mostly to Bellamy who listened through dense smoke and, from time to time, asked technical questions. Obviously, he neither knew much about the situation in Viet Nam nor did he seem to be interested. I was busy talking in Vietnamese with the hostess, mostly about food, complimenting her and enquiring about the ingredients.

As the dinner dragged on, Fred started to put his arm around my shoulders. I was a bit annoyed and embarrassed in front of the Vietnamese hosts.

"Listen, there is a medical military ship named HOPE coming to Saigon to work with the Vietnamese government. They are equipped with modern and up-to-date tools to service all ailments, especially tuberculosis and cancer." Fred turned to me and added: "I know the medics there. And of course we will be filming their work. Would you have any relative who needs to be looked at? I could help."

I had read about the medical ship "HOPE" the day before and did not pay too much attention. It was supposed to pay a friendly visit to Viet Nam for one week and would reciprocate the Vietnamese government's hospitality by agreeing to examine Vietnamese citizens with serious cases of tuberculosis or other incurable diseases on the ship. The idea had never entered my mind. Like anything else in Viet Nam, only influential and powerful politicians and high-ranking civil servants were allowed to profit by receiving special treatments.

My mother had suffered tuberculosis for several years and she lacked the correct treatment and medication. During her summer vacation, we took her to Dalat, the mountain resort city famous for its cool climate. The clean air and the serenity of the surroundings were well known for providing rest and repose to patients recovering from serious surgery or severe illness. HOPE, with experienced doctors on board, would be a godsend for my mother. I could at last learn more about my mother's definitive diagnosis. So I jumped at the offer.

"My mother has tuberculosis. She has been to several doctors and yet her health remains unstable." I told Fred.

"Oh, these medics are experts and your mother will be well taken care of. If you like, I can arrange an appointment for your mother tomorrow." I was overwhelmed with gratitude. At last, there was hope for my mother to get well.

The next day, Fred called to confirm the appointment for the following morning. "Listen, why don't you take your mother to the Caravelle hotel to rest for tomorrow's test. Take my room and I will move in with my team."

"It's very kind of you. I have to check with my mother although I don't want to disturb you," I answered lamely but very touched by his offer.

Of course, my mother was enchanted with the idea of being at the most famous and luxurious hotel. She had always loved luxury, high society and high class whenever the occasion arose. I could imagine her going back to Ben Tre with souvenirs from the Caravelle, boasting with her friends and colleagues about her daughter's influence and prestige in the government.

True to his word, Fred moved out and my mother occupied his room. That night, I put her to bed and left. In truth, my mother had the worst night. She was amazed by the surroundings. She enjoyed herself by touching and smelling the softness of the mattress, the decoration, the expensive furniture, by the whiteness of the curtains, and by the view. She couldn't believe that she herself was standing on the balcony of the most luxurious hotel to view Saigon at night when everything quieted down to almost stillness.

"It's too heavenly for me to sleep." I just wrapped my arms around her frail body and felt my emotions pouring out for her.

I accompanied her to the ship where Fred was waiting for us. I was not allowed in with her. HOPE had its own interpreter. By afternoon, I was called in to see the doctor. He confirmed that my mother's lungs were seriously affected and gave me various medications for her to take. Unfortunately, these American medics were not aware that these medications could not be obtained in Saigon. So once she finished the ones they gave her, there was no refill. She had to go back to her old doctor and continued to have shortness of breath and to be hospitalized several times. She died in March 1977.

HOPE left after a week and for several months, my mother seemed to be in good spirits. Two days after the visit to the ship, Fred called on my mother and met my family. My sister and her young children found him a good and handsome man.

"He looks very much like Fred McMurray, the American actor in the '50s," my sister said, and she was right. He was tall, had wavy short hair and was deeply tanned. He was funny and made everyone laugh with his awkward expressions when he tried to speak in broken French. He loved children, and my sister's children were fond of him. I went out with him a few times in the evening whenever his work freed him.

One evening, he called to ask whether I could come up to his room as he was about to finish a script draft. I was hesitant because the Caravelle was well guarded by security police. Fortunately, I was known there as staff of the Information Ministry. On several occasions, I made appointments to meet newcomers there to discuss their itinerary or to bring them back to see my minister.

Normally, I would never accept any invitation to meet someone in a hotel room. And up until that time, I only went out for a friendly dinner and no "hanky-panky", a new slang that the newsmen used to tease me with. I did not even hold hands with anyone. And that evening, somehow I consciously broke the rule. I could find many excuses to succumb to Fred's charm. For instance, he had respected me so far without making a pass at me.

And he was so kind to my mother and my family. It had been more than a year that I had broken off with my Vietnamese boyfriend. I needed affection, intimacy. I was in control of myself and liberated from all the social constraint. So I reasoned.

The evening ended, as I had suspected it would, in bed with Fred. I knew that I had not fallen in love with him. Whenever we were together, we only talked either about the situation in Viet Nam or about silly things. I recognized him as a playboy and also a married man. So why would I bother to ask about his life, knowing that he would be forced to lie. On the other hand, he never uttered a word either about his life, his work or his marital status.

Men usually liked to boast about their work or their family when they vent out with friends. I did not expect him to fall in love with me, either. It vas a physical attraction, or the pure joy of being free to make love. Fred might ave guessed or felt relieved that silently we understood one another. He left aigon a day or two later, and I resumed my normal life. There was always fear nd anguish that my behavior would catch up with me in the eyes of people at he Ministry. I was too close to the foreign press for comfort.

I was lucky to have an understanding boss, an expatriate like me. He vas also young and came from the South. We got along very well. I also susected that he also liked young and pretty women. He took me along as his ssistant to staff meetings and other official meetings. I sat next to him as he resided at his all-male staff meetings and with the male high-ranking officials oming from other ministries. I rode in the same car with him. I was asked to erve as hostess during official dinners given to visiting foreign dignitaries.

No one seemed to know whether my minister had divorced his French vife, or she preferred to live in France for a long period of time. In any case, I elt safe with him and shielded from the obnoxious Northern officials working round me. I became a permanent press relations officer. And I began to make riends with permanent residents of the foreign press corps. They often stopped y my office to chat. I was flattered and entertained by their activities. Some f them, perhaps, were looking for a pretext to cool their heels in an air-conditioned office. Others were really good friends.

François Nivolon was one of them. He was Malcolm's best man at our vedding. He was an old French journalist who had lived in Viet Nam since the rench had taken it back from the Japanese. He was, at that time, permanent orrespondent for the prestigious French daily "Le Figaro". Knowing that I poke fluent French, he would come in and tell me anecdotes of different sorts politics, gossip, people. He knew all the government members and all the /ietnamese elites in Saigon. He could bore me with his old stories for hours.

J. R. was another frequent visitor. He became a permanent freelancer or Time Magazine. He used to be a teacher in his home town, but he tired of eaching and came to Asia. He landed the freelancing job even without any experience in journalism. He came to tell me about his life. He ended up asking ne out.

J.R. was a young man, around 28, with blonde hair and blue eyes, fiveoot three. His home town was in upstate New York. He had graduated from public college with a degree in English. He was open and easy going. He mused me with his stories of growing up, or himself as a poor teacher living with his mother. He spoke fluent French and we discussed French literature and French jokes. We enjoyed one another's company. His salary was not high, but living in Saigon with US dollars was always beneficial, especially with a flourishing black market.

One morning, I was a bit annoyed to see him in my office, especially knowing that I had work to catch up on. He greeted me without smiling, sat down on the chair in front of my desk and remained silent.

"How was your trip yesterday," I asked while busily rearranging the files.

"I witnessed a crime of atrocities, yesterday." I looked up to see his grim face and his drawn features.

"Don't report what I am telling you to your boss. Otherwise, I'd be expelled. I saw with my own eyes the Vietnamese soldiers torturing a peasant in the rice field and shooting him. They then walked away while the Americans didn't do anything to help that poor man." He paused and looked at me in despair.

"I couldn't sleep the whole night."

"Was it your first time to see a dead body?"

"It was not dead bodies. It was atrocities and cruelties inflicted on these innocent peasants." He became agitated. "I don't know what to do. If I write the story, I may be expelled. And I don't want to upset this damned administration."

There was the truth in what he said. I knew some members of the foreign press had been expelled for some true but mildly insulting articles that the Diem regime disliked. They were banned from coming back for a long period of time, despite the intervention of their own government.

"So what are you going to do?"

"That's my problem. Let's go out and get drunk tonight, all right?"

R.J. ended up not writing the story. He did not even want to talk about it.

One day I was sick and stayed at home. In my semi-sleep, I heard someone knock on the door, which always remained open during the day time. I had my room upstairs. I heard footsteps climbing up, and raised my head to see J.R. coming up with a bouquet of flowers in his hands.

"How are you?" he approached my bed stretching out his arm with the flowers. "You don't have to get up." He looked around for a vase to put the flowers in. Seeing nothing, he just placed the flowers next to me.

"Hello, how did you know my address," I asked, surprised and annoyed at the same time. We lived in a blue-collar region where any slight departure from the usual norms was blown up into a rampage of gossip. And here I was alone, in bed with a "big nose," the insulting term for a white man.

"I called your office and they told me that you are sick. So I asked for the address and they gave it to me."

I was too sick to say anything.

"Would your reputation be destroyed by my presence here?" He looked so comic, towering above me with a concerned look on his face. I was touched by his kindness. "Your room is so empty. It's very clean but empty."

I had not even a chair where he could sit. I had a book shelf in which to put my books and music records that I had brought back from France, along with odds and ends. I used downstairs as the family living room for social occasions and took my meals there with my family. The living room became the bedroom at night where my two brothers slept.

"Is there anything you need that I can help with? Do you have anything to eat?"

"I can't eat anything. In any case, my sister will be here soon to cook for us."

"Do you live alone here?" I was alone that day.

"No, my two brothers live with me and they are at school. Would you like to sit down at the end of my bed?"

"No, I'll let you rest and see you tomorrow." He was standing there, silent and observant.

"Thank you for the flowers and for the visit. I'll be back to work tomorrow." I said stretching my arm to shake. He took it and kissed my hand and walked out.

I breathed with relief but unsettled. I never expected anyone to be kind to me. Not in that manner. "At last, I have a good male friend as I have always wished. Can that be?" I lay there with mixed emotions. Once more, I was pulled into a situation that I was too weak to resist.

I rarely had the time or money to read foreign newspapers. From time to time, some journalists would drop off their papers or forget them in my office. I also read their short cables whenever my boss did not like the words or phrases they contained. He wanted me to call the culprit in to protest or to threaten him. I had no idea what J.R. wrote except for what he told me. He also was very unhappy with Time.

"They badly edit what I write and at the end, it doesn't come out the way I wrote."

"I have heard this story from other journalists too," I tried to comfort him. "I suppose that everybody is in the same boat." By now, I was more or less in tune with what foreign correspondents were reporting about Viet Nam and the autocratic policies of Diem/Nhu. I was also part of the censorship of their cables, or rather served as an instrument to persuade the press to change words or paragraphs that the Minister didn't like. In turn, my boss just followed orders from the top of Viet Nam Press, the official spokesman of Diem/Nhu. I sympathized with J.R.

Since his visit at my home, I felt drawn closer to him. He was single and lonely in such an unwelcome place. He never mentioned his free-time activities. Through my social dinners with other journalists, I had learned that some of them did not like what he wrote and others rarely socialized with him enough to know him well. He confessed that he had no steady date, and only occasionally went out with an American secretary at the Embassy.

"You are my only date, you know that? You should know that I am very fond of you," he said, with tenderness and sincerity. I just looked down at my food, silent and moved. That was the evening after I had recovered from my sickness.

"I know that you like me," he went on. "Would you want to come to see where I live? I just moved into a new apartment not far from the old market."

"Is that an invitation for dinner?" I looked straight in his eyes. "Who is the cook?"

"I am a very good cook. I can even make good steaks with French fries," he smiled with pride. "How about tomorrow evening? It's Saturday."

J.R.'s apartment was located at the center of town, spacious with a big bright living room and modern Western-style kitchen. Two large windows opened onto a busy market called "cho cu" (old market). The only furniture was a small dining table fit for four persons with matching chairs and an enormous beige couch. The bedroom was smaller and windowless. It had only a double bed and a cabinet. Next to it was the average size bathroom built for foreigners with shower, a white sink and toilet bowl. In Vietnamese eyes, and especially in my eyes, the apartment was luxurious and expensive for one man. It had all the comfort that I had always dreamt of, but had no hope of owning.

"How beautiful your table is," I said, sincerely because J.R. had decorated it tastefully with white porcelain plates, small flowers and a white candle.

"I am going to fix you my special drink, a gimlet," he shouted from the kitchen.

"What's a gimlet?" I had never heard of that drink. At that time, I drank Campari, or Pernod, those French beverages. One time, someone ordered me a dry martini. And I liked it although I struggled to stand up afterwards.

"It's strong, so be careful," he warned me when he put the glass in front of me. I took a sip and immediately enjoyed the flavor and the taste.

True to his word, J.R. served me a big steak with salad and French bread. I didn't mention French fries out of courtesy and in truth I was never fond of potatoes. I finished my gimlet and began to feel a bit giddy.

"Would you would like some wine?" J.R. casually asked while he poured wine for both of us. I could not refuse because I always liked red wine with my meal, a habit I acquired in France. I did not remember our conversation except that by the time I was served coffee, my face had turned purple and my words were slurred. (It's a trait that all Vietnamese turn red-faced after drinking alcohol. It was mostly embarrassing for men. Women rarely drink.)

I must have said something funny or stupid that made J.R. laugh. He took me in his arms and kissed me on the mouth. I returned the kiss and we ended up in each other's arms in bed.

After our passionate love making, I felt sleepy as the time drew late.

"Why don't you stay overnight here," he suggested. I had never been away from home at night unless I was out of town on mission. I thought of my mother, who had just came up for the week-end. We were too poor to afford a telephone. But I was not so sure that I was steady enough to go outside. Finally, I succumbed to sleep.

I woke very early in the morning, trying to get up when J.R. pulled me down and we made love once more.

Once I was in the taxi, I tried to make up a story to cover my absence that night.

"Where have you been?" my mother asked, giving me an anxious look as soon as I got to the door.

"I was with Mai and Hung (the couple who were friends back when we were students in France and we continued to see each other In Saigon) and it was too late, so they asked me to stay overnight."

Mai and Hung lived at the outskirts of Saigon and very often I was invited to dine with them at home. My mother did not say anything further and I congratulated myself for such a lie.

After that, I would meet J.R. at his apartment after work. We went out for dinner and came home to make love. We were discreet and just enjoyed one another's company. I believed that he sincerely loved me although we never discussed any future between us.

One day, I innocently asked him whether it was wise to make love when I had my period. He gave me a sad look and said:

"It's too bad. I was expecting you to be pregnant when I realized that you were overdue for the last two weeks. Imagine how beautiful our child would be with our mixed blood." I was stunned and speechless.

"Do you really mean it?" I thought he was making fun of me.

"Of course, it would give me a chance to marry you." He put his arm around my waist and kissed me on the cheek. I did not venture further. If he loved me that much, there was no reason for him to wait for me to be pregnant. On the other hand, I was very fond of him, but ambiguous in my emotions.

Ever since I grew up, I kept telling myself that I never trusted men and their fidelity. I saw all around me, married men, especially Vietnamese men, constantly cheating on their wives. In Vietnamese culture, men could have as many concubines as they could afford or as many as their wives would tolerate. My own dearest father whom I adored and worshipped, cheated on my mother at least once. I learned that only late in life when I asked her.

So our love affair smoothly sailed along for several months. Meanwhile, I continued to go out with casual "dates" as before. J.R. did not fuss, knowing that he had no hold on me and at the same time that it was part of my job. We respected each other's independence and never questioned our loyalty towards one another. Life in Saigon was still calm and peaceful. One heard of skirmishes in the Delta or a few villages that had been attacked by the Viet Cong and then retaken by government troops, the ARVN (Army of the Republic of Viet Nam.) Few foreign journalists came until the end of 1961.

November 10 was my birthday, and that day my sister and her husband gave a party for me at a night club along the Saigon River. Her best friend was also invited. By midnight, Philippe drove us along the Nguyen Hue Boulevard. We noticed troops in full gear popping in and out of the bushes planted in the center of the road.

"What's going on?" Philippe wondered.

"Probably we were going to have a big parade tomorrow, November 11,th for Armistice Day." I contributed my opinion. He dropped me at my house and I immediately went upstairs to sleep. As soon as I dozed off, I heard gun shots and cannon explosions. My mother, who had come up for my birthday and slept downstairs with my brothers, yelled up for me to come down. I was too tired to pay attention.

The next day, we learned that it was a coup d'État that had gone badly vrong. A group of so-called Southern nationalists supported by a few Southern nilitary officers thought that the troops would rally with them to take over the egime. (The rebel leader turned out to be my mother's boyfriend when she vas young - a surprise revelation on the part of my mother. The rebels were aptured and jailed. I don't remember what happened to them after that.)

The event drew the foreign press back to Viet Nam. I was inundated by ournalists from all over the world coming to be accredited. Diem's cabinet was eshuffled. The Viet Nam Press took over responsibility for handling news and he foreign press. New faces were brought in to deal with the crowd of international journalists. I was asked to continue working in press relations under he supervision of a group of expatriates whom I had never met before. They vere young men in their early 30s who had studied in the States. They treated ne as part of their group. I even received some bonus money for my work that vas taken from their special funds. The funds were very helpful and roused my nthusiasm. For once, I felt that I was appreciated. Many familiar faces greeted ne with friendly hugs. Among them was Fred R. of NBC.

And so was Malcolm W. Browne, the new AP Bureau Chief replacing ohn Griffin. Malcolm arrived on November 11, 1961.

CHAPTER FOUR

Life often played tricks at the most unexpected time.

My relationship with J.R. continued smoothly. We enjoyed one another's company. We could relax and be as casual as any ordinary married couple. We never touched on the subject of love. J.R was kind and considerate. Short for an American, he had wavy blond hair, a "profiled" nose and thin lips. His baby face and white complexion promised gentility and mild manner. He was not like the rest of the foreign press, and seemed like a lost child in this aggressive and competitive group. He was tender and vulnerable. My feelings towards J.R. were complex, a kind of "wait and see." Then came Fred.

"Are you going out with him?" J.R. brought up the subject as soon as he heard that Fred had arrived in town.

I was taken back. So far, I was free to go out for dinner with anyone I wanted to. That was our understanding -- that it was part of my job, and what I wanted. His question irritated my ego.

"Yes, if he asks me," I answered defiantly. He remained silent and broody.

Fred did call me, and we were back as lovers again. I had hurt J.R. He did not call or look me up. Fred took me to Vung Tao, a white-sand beach resort about 100 kilometers northeast of Saigon. He also rented a house in Saigon for some days to be with me. He showered me with gifts and attention. I was amused and savored these feckless moments.

I could find tens of excuses to justify my "libertine" behavior. For instance, I was too young and too vain to bow to any man. My boring life made me do outrageous or scandalous things to break away from tradition and correctness. Or, simply, I liked challenge and competition. In truth, I wanted to enjoy life regardless of future consequences or bad gossip.

Back in the '50s and early '60s, Viet Nam was still under the influence of Confucius, and especially under the influence of the Northern refugees who had fled the North after partition in 1954 had left it communist. They came with their own particular kind of morality. In a northerner household in the South, young brides had to agree in advance, before marriage, to live with their in-laws as domestic household help, cooking, cleaning, mothering and obeying the commands of their husband's parents. In the South, women were treated as equal to their husbands, having their own occupation and living in a separate home with husband and children if they could afford it.

Fortunately, I had an understanding and free-spirited mother who always supported me, right or wrong. Grown up in the West, I inherited some of the Westerners' culture and the women's liberation movement. I did not consider having an affair with a man as a sin, as long as both respected each other. With Fred, it was just a passing divertissement. I knew nothing about his marital status, as he never mentioned it. For sure, Fred was a womanizer and a playboy, and so I considered him a play-pal, probably with multiple affairs with women at every corner of the world. I did not feel that I was stealing someone's husband. That was always "forbidden territory" under my strict rule. To me, it was cruel and cheap to mix it up with married men. My dates with married journalists were pure friendship. My conscience was clear.

Anyway, after ten days in Saigon, Fred left and we lost contact. I also lost contact with J.R. Neither of us tried to communicate with the other. It was fair and even. I missed his company, but neither felt ashamed nor regretted my behavior. Psychologically, I was scared of succumbing to love, and of later disappointment if J.R. and I remained together. I needed to confront my own insecurity and stood on my self-sufficiency. Besides, I naïvely and romantically believed that if one was sincerely in love, one had to make every effort to prove it. J.R. did not want to get into that kind of game. I was very fond of J.R. and yet did not see my future with him. So we both, with mutual consent, avoided one another. I had my job to keep me busy, and soon I tumbled into Malcolm W. Browne.

As I had predicted, Malcolm asked me out a week after I had met him and processed his requests. We went out for dinner and went to the Majestic hotel sidewalk café for a drink. During our conversation, he told me that he was married and just had a baby of two months. They were going to join him in Saigon after he settled down and found an apartment.

"I congratulate you for your new baby," I said cheerfully. "He must be very cute at that age. How does your family feel about living in Viet Nam?"

"She is my second wife," Malcolm quipped, blowing cigarette smoke from a corner of his mouth. I was shocked. He looked so young, not more than 23 or 24, to have already had two wives. Actually he was 30. I gazed at his face, handsome with fine features. His mouth was wide with full lips. But he chain-smoked, a habit that I tremendously disliked and disapproved of.

"I see. I hope that you are happy now, and especially with a new baby," I said, enthusiastically, to be sociable. Most men I went out with were married or had girl-friends and they were usually frank and proud to tell me about their family. The way Malcolm phrased his words raised my suspicion. I wondered if he had heard someone bad-mouthing me and so wanted to warn me about his status.

"How do you like it here?' I changed the subject. "It sounded like you went through an awful experience with the Vietnamese military operation. I come from that region."

"Do you? It's a very beautiful region."

"It's famous for its political inclination towards the Viet Cong and for beautiful girls."

"Now I know why it's beautiful," he joked. (Malcolm vividly described his trip to the Delta in his book "Muddy Boots and Red Socks: A Reporter's Life," first published by Times Books/Random House in 1993, pp.107-108.)

"To answer your question," he continued, "I had a very hellish day there that I will never forget as long as I live."

"Was it that bad?" He told me the story. "Well, you are now safe and it's such a beautiful evening."

I sat back to enjoy the freshness of the evening. The Majestic hotel was built by the French along the Saigon River. I never had any occasion to step inside the hotel, and now I had an opportunity to quickly glimpse inside before settling down in one of the tables outside. The lobby was brightly lit and outfitted with French furniture. Luxurious shops had decorated the walls with tasteful and expensive imported products. I liked the wide dimly-lit outdoor café, quiet, serene and so romantic. The view of the wide river in the evening produced vivid emotions in me. Darkly lit sampans silently sliding along the current, as if unmanned and ghostly. Their oil lights flickered in the air as if they were communicating with the stars above. (Sampan is a French word describing a big canoe with a thatched roof in the middle, serving as the owner's quarters.) The sky was littered with billions of blinking stars. Through the flamboyant trees, their reflections looked like mini dancing mermaids on the water.

"I had the happiest ride in one of these sampans when I was a child," I said, moved by the sight and the memories of the happy boat trip that I had made with my mother and my siblings at night. (see chapter 3)

"Was it nice?" Malcolm's eyes lit up. "Tell me about it." I told him about that trip. He put his hand on mine on the table and silently smoked his cigarette with the other hand. I thought of my poor father, wherever he was. (I stayed at that luxurious Majestic hotel during Christmas 2016. Unfortunately the sidewalk café didn't exist anymore, replaced by a parking lot for taxis and limousines. The large two-lane boulevard in front of the hotel was congested with thousands of motorcycles and cars, honking, puttering smoke and inching forward. The air was hazy with the pollution and fumes of thousands of vehicles that passed by 24/7, and there was the deadening noise of traffic and crowds of people. All of this effaced the tranquility and serenity of the old days, in my eyes.)

That evening was my first meeting with Malcolm. He impressed me as a young man who had come to look for adventure. He spoke French and was eager to show off his knowledge of the Vietnamese language: "queo tay trai, queo tay mat" (turn left, turn right,) enough to give direction to taxi drivers, to quote him. His first articles on his trip to the Delta were not favorably received by my Ministry. I did not tell him that. I never disclosed what I had learned in the office when I went out with newsmen except to listen to their complaints or opinions.

Being a permanent member of the foreign press corps, Malcolm would occasionally see me for various reasons relating to his work. In between, he kept calling me and inviting me out almost every weekend. I expected his wife and baby come to join him any moment.

The situation in Saigon, after the failed coup, became more critical. The personalist cult of the leadership became more evident. We, as civil servants, were often ordered to line up on the street early in the morning, whenever the ministry learned that President Diem's motorcade would pass by on his way to the airport or to visit hamlets outside Saigon. We were supposed to cheer him and his "clique" by waving the paper yellow and red flag of the Republic of Vietnam and shouting out the slogan "Ung ho Tong Thong" (loosely translated, "Long Live the President.") Political meetings proliferated, and Mme Nhu reinforced her power by creating her own female paramilitary group. Rumors of arrests and tortures went viral. The government began to increase the military draft. My youngest brother was called up. Corruption was rampant. You could pay to bail out a loved one from the draft. You paid under the table for a better job, for an exit visa, for traffic accidents, to see big shots, for almost everything and anything. Meantime, traveling outside Saigon became dangerous as the Viet Cong increased their harassments and kidnappings. Daily news of military and civilian casualties threatened the stability of the nation. The foreign press corps also expanded from a handful to dozens strong. I was busier than ever. I forgot J.R., until one day, I ran into him in the street.

I had not seen him for over a month after Fred left. I was so pleased to see him that "it showed all over my face", according to his remark later. We went out for dinner that day and went back to his apartment.

"I am seeing a woman," he told me after we made love. "It's bizarre to love two women at the same time."

"Are you serious?" I casually asked. "Who is she?"

"She is American, a secretary at the American Embassy," he answered. "I'd have loved to marry you if you were not involved with Fred." He kissed my neck as I was dressing. I obviously felt hurt and humiliated. But, I did not blame him, nor was I jealous. After all, I had provoked the rupture.

"Did you tell her about us?" I asked with concern.

"I thought it was over between us," he said as he wrapped his hands around my waist. "I just mentioned your name, but I don't think she knows."

"Then, we should stop seeing one another," I said. He turned silent and went to the refrigerator to pour a drink. I watched his face, tight-lipped and angry. I slipped out without a word.

Once more, we parted without any further hope of meeting again. He didn't even come to my office. And I did not try to find out what had become of him. Then, one day, long after our separation, J.R. came to my home one Saturday afternoon as I was about to step out.

"Let's go back to the house," he said, taking my arm and pushing me inside, serious and unsmiling.

"Is anything wrong?" I stared at him, a bit concerned.

"I am getting married next week."

"Oh! With the same secretary?" I breathed with relief.

"Yes, we have been seeing one another a lot lately and she is good for me." He looked at me, still unsmiling and expecting something from me.

"Congratulations. When's the wedding? Am I invited?"

"No. It's a small party with friends."

"Well, I wish you and your future wife a lot of happiness." I kissed him on the cheek. He held me in his arms briefly.

"Are you all right?" he asked, his eyes fixed on me.

"Yes, I have to go. I am late." I was sad, but happy for him.

By the time I met J.R. again, he and his wife just had a first baby. By then I was seriously involved with Malcolm. I did not know and still don't know whether Malcolm was aware of my relationship with J.R. If he was, he never gave any hint. On the other hand, J.R. told him about my affair with Fred when Malcolm was on vacation in Hong Kong. Malcolm trusted me and loved me as I was. Fred did come back to Viet Nam a third time, but I turned down his invitation then to go for a cup of coffee in our office cafeteria.

J.R. quit being a journalist and somehow got hired by the Vietnamese Ministry of the Interior. He told me that one day in 1963 when he came to see me when I was working in the American information office, the Joint United States Public Affairs Office, JUSPAO). He wanted me to come and work for him. I categorically turned down the offer, not because of our relationship, but because I had come out of the frying pan and did not want to jump back into the fire. I was not even interested to know what kind of job J.R. held.

Malcolm and I continued to see J.R. after that, and occasionally had dinner with him. On one occasion, his wife happened to be in town. We, all four, went out for a meal, the first time I met her – I forget her name. She was petite, shy and quiet. She spoke little but seemed at ease in my presence. I felt convinced that he had made a good choice .

J.R. and I became good friends and confidants. He loved and missed his children, living with their mother in Hong Kong. He felt that Saigon could no longer guarantee security for the children after the My Canh, an open floating restaurant on the Saigon River, was blown up in 1965. It was very popular with foreign visitors because its cuisine was a mix of famous Vietnamese dishes and genuine French gourmet dishes. And it was an attractive and romantic location, with its hanging lanterns swinging in the dark. It offered peace and tranquility to young couples who came to enjoy privacy and coolness. Malcolm and I went there often, although it was pricey for modest families. The Viet Cong blew it up one evening with Claymore mines, killing some 40 clients, mostly Americans and well-off Vietnamese families. One particular American and his pregnant Vietnamese wife with whom Malcolm was friends were among the casualties.

"I fear for my family's safety; we used to go and eat at My Canh," J.R. told me. "I can't help but think that we might have been casualties ourselves."

His apprehension was prophetic. Later that year, I received a telephone call from a Vietnamese friend who worked for ABC. She informed me that an Air Viet Nam plane had been shot down and that J.R., his boss the Minister of Interior, and other passengers had been killed. In panic, I called Malcolm, who was not aware of the news. He called me back with confirmation. I had lost the dearest friend, the best and only male friend, not lover, that I had always dreamt to have. I thought of his wife and wished she were in Saigon so that I could take her in my arms and console her. He left his wife and two young children with very little savings. Malcolm was asked by his wife to take care of J.R.'s remains and to send his ashes by air-freight back to his family in Hong

Kong. I went with Malcolm to retrieve the urn. It was a black day I will never forget. Malcolm drove me back to my office first, with J.R.'s urn between us. I put my hand on it and cried. I still visualize his smiling face and miss him very much.

Even now, I cannot help but keep thinking that somehow fate or destiny or simply intuition had driven me away from J.R. I could have been his wife and his widow at such a young age with two young children to raise. Malcolm used to call me "femme fatale." I was obsessed that death and grief sooner or later would fall upon me. I lived in fear of losing my mother, who was sick and getting old. After I had lived with Malcolm, whenever he went out on a military operation, I visualized myself receiving news of his death at any moment. All through our life together, covering many wars, I constantly lived in fear of losing Malcolm. I was raised as a traditional Buddhist, but I was non-practical and yet very religious when I sensed some danger hovering around me, praying until the danger passed. In the end, we did have a rich life, as Malcolm had felt we would all along.

A lot of friends and people whom Malcolm and I met during our wandering life always asked me how we met.

"I guess you both fell in love right away?" That was the common question/self-answer I heard from everybody's mouth.

"He was already married," I would say, leaving the rest for them to guess. I self-consciously felt sensitive about it, because I had never intended to break-up anyone's marriage. I had mentioned that before; it was my own dogma. I liked to go out with him because he truly cared about my country and wanted to know more about its culture and customs. Most foreign journalists were more interested in the war and our politics than in our culture and customs.

Every time Malcolm and I met, I took him to the zoo or to other places that Vietnamese people frequented. I told him about my anti-communist sentiments and my disappointment with the government. I explained Vietnamese jokes, slang and curses, and he, in turn, liked to tease me with bad jokes. He also used what he learned from me in his writing. I was impressed by his seriousness about learning and trying to adjust to the hostility of the natives towards white people.

I began to know more about the way of life in the States. Malcolm talked a lot about the country and his personal hobbies and interests. He lived for classical music. When he came, there was nothing to show of American influence. The radio was either in Vietnamese or French, with tear-jerking Vietnamese melodies or popular French music.

In 1962, when the Kennedy administration decided to increase the number of American advisors and later kept increasing the military buildup, the Americans had their own radio station, broadcasting in English. In Malcolm's book, he thoroughly researched and described in detail all the new weapons and airplanes provided to the Vietnamese armed forces. Years later, he kept himself up-to-date with all newly fabricated modern weaponry used to fight the first war in the Persian Gulf and later. His vast knowledge of all kinds of armory dated back to his childhood fascination with chemistry and explosives.

Malcolm was fanatic about World War II and the Spanish Civil War, especially the aviation side. He bought WWII airplane kits and spent his leisure time researching and building these kits from scratch. Most of his airplanes from Germany, Japan, Spain and Britain were carefully chosen for their valiant fights during the war.

He studiously painted the camouflage, the signs, and the logos as described specifically in the series of books "War Planes of The Second World War" by William Green. He was so proud of his model airplanes, and even let me hold them. One day, I casually picked up one of these models to admire the painting on it, when I clumsily snapped a wheel. His face became red and without a word, he took the plane from my hands and put it back in the box along with the others. I had committed a crime in his eyes.

Another time, Malcolm had just bought a new remote control airplane which was very expensive from the PX in Saigon, the store reserved for American military personnel, and was so proud and excited that he took me to Tan Son Nhat airport to try it out. The heat was intense at midday. Standing in the middle of nowhere without any tree for shade, he launched his airplane and nervously worked on the remote control, forgetting me and the whole surrounding. He was a kid again with his favorite toy. It was an endearing sight to watch. He then gave it to me to try out. I refused because I was sweating and was frying in that heat. But he kept insisting, I crashed and destroyed the plane at first try. We went back to town in silence.

For me, these outings were innocent and enjoyable. I also learned a lot about his life, his family, New York and America. He introduced me to some typical American food such as canned baked beans, Campbell's soups, hot dogs, and of course hamburgers. I never did acquire a taste for canned beans.

One day he declared that he loved me and wanted to marry me.

"Come on, you are married," I laughed. "Aren't your wife and baby coming?"

He showed me a telegram. “I just received it today,” he said grimly.

“Plan to come…,” I forgot the rest. His wife had cabled him her intention of arriving in Saigon at such and such a date.

“So here you are!” I said cheerfully, not knowing how to react.

“I don’t want her to come,” Malcolm said, tight-lipped. I looked at him in astonishment. He did tell me that his marriage with his second wife had been a mistake, forced to give the baby legitimacy. But, of course, I knew, every married man keen on an extra-marital affair always recited the same song. I had read in books, heard with my own ears and seen many broken families. Malcolm was a very good looking man, intelligent and well-bred. During all our outings, we never held hands or had any physical touch. I always looked upon him as a friend and learned companion.

“You know that I am not fooling with married men,” I looked him in the face, and continued: “I don’t believe what you say.”

“I was in love with you the first day we met,” he said blowing out smoke from his mouth. I was out of words and felt utterly out of place. “I am going to stop her from coming.”

Two days later, he came to my house and showed me the telegram in which he told his wife not to come. “If you insist on coming, I can arrange for you to have your own place to live.” I didn’t finish the cable. I handed it back to him, speechless and horrified. That was how I had imagined bad married men would behave -- vile, cruel and senseless. How could he abandon his family, especially a small baby, for me? Yet deep down, I appreciated his gentleness and honesty.

“Now, you believe me?” Malcolm triumphantly voiced, bending down to look at my face.

“She is going to come anyway,” I said, confronted by my own conscience.

“No, she won’t,” he retorted firmly. “I know her.”

“I have to meet some Americans now, I’ll call you later.” Malcolm rushed out. I was so glad to see him leave. I was at a loss. I only wished that he was wrong and that his wife would come anyway, threat or no threat. After all, Saigon was not that dangerous then. And she was a reporter in her own right, so Malcolm told me before; she might even find some free-lancing job here. I was convinced that she had already made up her mind and was all packed up ready to go; there was no reason for her to stop. I knew about his wife only what he had told me. That was not very much to begin with. But I would be surprised if she should give up so easily.

I was wrong again. A few days later, Malcolm showed me another cable. His wife had decided to stay where she was. I felt trapped and questioned my own feelings towards Malcolm. I was flattered to be loved by such a handsome young man whom I guessed many women might have loved to possess.

I had been with Malcolm for months now. He was courting me so intensely that I never had a moment to think of dating anyone else. My weekends were booked with him, along with other evenings of the week. The news of her not coming at all sent me into a profound reflection about what to do. Up until then, I had never thought deeply about love, nor would I advance any intention of loving him. Before I could say or react, Malcolm said:

"I promise you that I will marry you as soon as I get the divorce." He took me in his arms and gave me the most passionate kiss, and that sealed my fate. I felt love flowing in my veins, perforating my self-defense mechanisms and bringing down my own moral myth. No one had ever proposed marriage to me before. One thing for sure was that Malcolm's love for me was sincere and unquestionable. I began to seriously consider my future with him. From that day on, I felt like a different woman, fulfilled and liberated. All my suspicions, self-reservation and insecurity flew out the window. Now we openly and officially began going out as a couple with our friends and acquaintances. I introduced him to my mother and my siblings. What I failed to mention to them was that Malcolm was married.

True to his word, Malcolm asked his wife for a divorce. He explained to me that divorce was not easy in New York. It might take a long time, years even. However, if his wife did not contest it, she could go to the Mexican border where divorce was granted within 24 hours or so.

I continued in my job. From time to time, I was asked to accompany foreign officials and diplomats to various places where President Diem wanted to show off success and achievements. On these occasions, I was often offered a job at various embassies. But I had signed a three-year contract with the government, which would never let me go. Even a friend of mine who happened to work for the Vietnamese Foreign Affairs ministry failed when he tried to get me a job with the Vietnamese Embassy to the French Congo. That had been a big disappointment. One day, during one of my field trips, an Australian diplomat told me that Australian Broadcasting Corporation (ABC) was considering adding a Vietnamese-language version to their international broadcast, the "Voice of Australia." He wanted me to apply when they started recruiting. I was flattered but sadly said, "I don't believe that I could be relieved from my commitment to the Information Ministry."

"You never know," he said, sure of himself. I brushed the idea aside. There was no point for me in torturing myself; besides, by then Malcolm and I vere too deep in for me to think of leaving him. We were waiting for his wife's iews about the divorce. A month or so, the long awaited cable arrived when I vas with Malcolm: his wife was refusing to give him the divorce.

"I'll hire a lawyer and believe me, I'll win," Malcolm said, wrapping iis two hands around his nose and violently shaking his head. By now, I rec- ognized his twitter: his personal expression of emotional agitation or anger. I eceived the news with no surprise and was ready to give up. Call it what you night: kismet, femme fatale, psyche. That's part of my predestinate stigma; all vritten in the sky. All I could do was to accept and tumble on, come what may.

A few days after the divorce news, I was walking to my office when I an into the Australian diplomat again. He approached me and said: "The ABC lirector is here now and is recruiting staff for the new Vietnamese program. Are you going to apply?"

"I have no hope of success. My boss wouldn't relieve me," I casually inswered.

"Do go and apply. You never know." His voice was insistent and firm. was impressed.

"All-right! I need the address." He took out his business card and scrib- bled the address on the reverse side.

"Good luck!" he waved good-bye, smiling.

I called ABC when I got back to my office. I got an appointment the iext day, in the afternoon. It was Saturday. I was to meet Malcolm for brunch t his apartment. I still had not decided to go for the interview that afternoon. n my mind, luck was never in my vocabulary. Besides having no hope of being ermitted to leave my job, I had no experience in radio – and thousands of qualified Vietnamese who badly wanted to get out of the country might have better opportunity.

"I have to work this afternoon," Malcolm said as we ate. "What are you going to do? You can stay in the apartment and wait for me."

"Oh, in that case, I can always go for a job interview with radio Aus- ralia." I wearily answered.

"What radio Australia? Isn't that the one that ABC plans to start Viet- namese language broadcasting?" Malcolm frowned at me.

"Yes, I've promised my Australian friend to go for an interview. I am pretty certain that I would not be qualified. But what the heck! I have nothing lse to do this afternoon." I said, waving my hands in the air.

"The bastard!" Malcolm knew the Australian diplomat , Tony Neylan.

"I bet that you get the job. I am sure that you will get the job. Do you want to go to Australia?" he asked me, with anger in his voice.

"Don't worry. I have no chance. A lot of qualified Vietnamese have already applied for just five openings. Even if I get the job, my boss wouldn't let me go anyway. You should know that." I was a bit annoyed by his tone of voice

"Australia is a friend of Diem's administration. Diem would be delighted to do some small favor for their friend," he answered.

"Oh yeah?" I fired back. "Do you know that, a few months ago, I was offered a job working at the Vietnamese Embassy in French Congo by an influential friend at the Vietnamese Foreign Affairs Ministry, and you know what? They refused to let me go. So I know that I have no chance to go anywhere." I began to feel sorry for myself.

We parted that afternoon in a gloomy mood. I dragged myself to the Australian Office in downtown Saigon. Being so indifferent to the whole thing, I don't remember the interview or the interviewer himself – I must have taken everything in stride. I was relaxed and light-hearted. All I remembered was that they asked me whether I would still be willing to take a job as an administration officer if the speaker jobs were taken. I was willing to take any job, I said light-heartedly. The interview was short and I left with the feeling that the interviewer met me out of obligation to my Australian friend's recommendation. I brushed aside the whole thing as a joke and appreciated my friend's good intention.

Two weeks later, I was summoned to see the minister of Civic Action, Mr. Ngo Trong Hieu, whose responsibility included the Ministry of Information. Hearing his name gave me a chill and terror in my heart. Hieu was famous as a womanizer and a bon vivant. He was close to the Diems' regime and shared power with the Diems' secret service. I had met him on some trips with foreign dignitaries, but never approached him.

A rotund big man, uncommon for a Vietnamese man, he was in his 60s, ugly with very dark skin, almost more Cambodian than Vietnamese. He was sitting at a huge desk at the end of an enormous spacious office, a cigar in his mouth. He looked up when I stepped in.

"Come in, Miss Le Lieu," he leant back on his enormous chair looking down from his eyeglasses. I slowly tiptoed across that big space between the door and his desk. He pointed to a chair in front of his desk for me to sit down. Next to this big man, I felt small and timid.

"So you want to go to work with radio Australia?" he spoke in French, ooking at me and smiling. I was abashed. I had completely forgotten about Australia or the job. I did not count on hearing from them, and had not even bothered to contact them, figuring that it was a lost cause in advance. So as Malcolm had predicted, the Australian government directly contacted Mr. Hieu, who, in turn, passed on the news to me. There was nothing I could do but nod affirmatively. Did I cause some embarrassment to the ministry? Or was I accused of betraying the ministry by secretly applying for the job? I was glued to my chair; my mouth was dry, expecting a sermon and a refutation. I lowered my eyes and stayed silent.

"In principle, I would not let you go as you are under contract for three years with the government." He paused, puffing on his cigar and smiled at me.

"On the other hand, you were very kind with my daughter. You saved her life. I am very grateful." He softly spoke in a fatherly voice. I looked at him in surprise and puzzled at the same time.

"Come out, dearest," he called out, then got up and rounded the desk towards the other end of the room. I also got up and slowly turned around to look. A young woman in black "ao dai" silently slid out from behind the curtain, shyly smiling and moving towards me. I recognized her immediately and with joy I came towards her and we hugged. I had not seen or heard of her for years - since I left the convent in England where we both were boarders and students learning English back in mid '50s.

Julie had not changed. She had her father's dark skin, long straight hair down to the waist, and the same smile and soft and gentle voice that I remembered. She was much younger than I. In fact, she was only 16 when I met her in the convent. We were only two Asians among some twenty European students coming to Watergate-on-Sea in Cornwall to study English after high-school graduation. She was the youngest and was always lonely and broody. I regarded her as my younger sister and spent a lot of time with her to keep her company. She confided to me of her intention of entering a Catholic order as a novice. I was upset not at her but at the nuns in the convent. Their great ambition was to convert young students into their fold. Two Vietnamese women fell under their influence and became devout Catholics, attending mass twice a day. The religious tried on me, a non-believer in any religion. Every day, I was scolded by the reverend mother that I could learn English better if I attended Mass.

She tried to isolate me from everyone who wanted to be friendly with me - students and teachers (all religious novices and nuns), and even au-pair students who exchanged work for tuition and boarding. Ironically, these latter became and still remain my best friends up to the present time. My friends dared not tell me about their working there for fear of being dismissed. I only learned after we quit the convent.

To think back, the reverend mother might have forbidden Julie to befriend me too. That might have pulled her closer to me because we were compatriots. Julie was a devout Catholic, but also was Vietnamese and looked upon me as a big sister who understood her better than any foreigner - especially when her English was still too poor to communicate her feelings to strangers.

Julie was homesick and alone without any close relatives at her side. She did tell me something about her father's holding a very important job in Vietnam. I had been away for too many years to know who was who in Viet Nam at that time. I worried about her. She was just a teenager, abandoned in such a gloomy environment, without her family. It was a difficult and tender age to be left without any friends.

We were drawn together because both of us were strangers in the school. In those years, Asians (including Vietnamese) were a rare breed in rural England. Now the Asian population has fast grown to become one of the multiple cultures in British society.

Julie and I sometimes shared an Asian meal in my room. English repasts were not our favorite and we were constantly hungry. During these get-togethers Julie would have told me about her life, her homesickness and finally her decision to enter the order. I pounded on her about her future and her responsibility to her family. I appealed to her to think of her father who had sacrificed for her by sending her to study in Europe.

I don't remember much what we did or talked about together during that year. My only aim was to convince her to abandon the idea of becoming a nun. I was not sure how effective my words were. I was not convinced that my influence was strong enough for her to pay heed after my departure. I only feared that once I was gone she would be back in the grip of these religious.

And now, here was Julie, looking so smart and yet still shy in front of me. I was so pleased to see an old face from the past. Ever since I had returned from Europe, I lost contacts with old friends except for these two best friends I had mentioned above. Julie outgrew her bad dream and now was back in the family bosom. The man standing in front of me no longer seemed like an imposing bully official, but rather a simple tender father.

I was so moved that no word came out of my throat. We hugged and laughed. We whispered incoherent greetings and held hands. It was such a stunning surprise to learn that she was the daughter of such an important high-ranking official. I babbled polite and meaningless words to her while, in

ruth, I meant to enquire about her present life and family – these silly ques-
ions that friends ask one another after a long absence.

Mr. Hieu watched us, laughing and applauding. He then went to the lesk, signed the paper, and handed it to me.

"We will miss you," Hieu sighed and interrupted us. I clapped my two ands together, a formal Buddhist greeting, and bowed. He extended his hand nd shook mine. "You'll arrange the time and paperwork with your boss. I wish ou good luck."

I hugged Julie and walked out, carefully rolling the important docu-nent and tightly tugging it in my purse. I could not describe my emotions at hat moment. I was staggering out onto the sidewalk, dazed and thrilled. I was n angel – me! an angel, a doer of good deeds, and now I was rewarded! I was valking on water, smiling and dreaming. Fairy tales did exist; I was Cinderella vho was freed at last from the grip of the ogre, in the form of the authoritarian egime.

And Australia! The country suddenly popped up on my imaginative nap as an invisible city surging out of nowhere in one of the illustrations of the ame fairy tale. How did it all happen? I looked up in the sky. It was cloudless nd brilliant. '"Up there, someone has arranged my life for me," I murmured or myself. "Thank you Heaven."

Within two hours, my life turned "topsy-turvy." It was unpredicted nd I was unprepared, and yet impetuously stirred toward another direction. What I had considered as a whimsical action taken with a grain of salt, apply-ng for the job, had turned into factual reality

I went back to my office and called ABC. They were pleased to hear hat I was released from my contract and affirmatively confirmed my job. They vere preparing letters to go out for all accepted candidates and to fix a meeting vith all of us for the week after. I met with my boss between his busy schedules o announce my resignation. I handed him Mr. Hieu's letter. He briefly glanced t it and set it aside.

"When do you plan to leave," he asked with slight irritation.

"According to the ministry regulations, I have to let you know two veeks in advance." I sheepishly answered. I had been dreaming of the day I vould quit this office from the first day I started, more than a year and a half arlier. Yet, I must confess that the job gave me so many opportunities to meet vith the whole range of professionals, civil servants, foreign press and foreign lignitaries. Despite the authoritarian regime and the war, I was launched into whirlwind of learning, groping and growing up in a world rich with knowledge, intrigues, and adventures. Now, I was giving up all this to move on to new and still unknown ground.

Australia, down under, was and still is a member of the British Commonwealth. The country was created by British convicts and turned into one of the most advanced and modern in South Asia. Australian troops were sent to Viet Nam to support their ally, the United States. So I was not going to some savage place to work. I knew that much. I had the opportunity to explore a new continent.

I told the news to my family that evening and they were all excited for me and even envious of my good fortune.

"Luck seems to go with you. It's written in your hands," my mother quietly stated. She strongly believed on astrology and witchcraft. "We may have a chance to go and live in Australia once you make a lot of money."

"I'd like to go and live with you as soon as you are settled down," my sister burst out enthusiastically. I thought she must be depressed. Something must be wrong at home. She and her husband constantly fought whenever he was at home. She clung to the family for moral support although she never talked much about her problems. She was in her 8th month of her third pregnancy. France and Dominique ("Nique") were 4 and almost 3 years old. Our whole family adored the children and spoiled them whenever they came to visit us.

"Of course, I believe that I'll become an Australian citizen and send for you all," I said cheerfully.

"Did Malcolm know?" my mother suddenly interrupted my thoughts.

"No! I haven't seen him today." I had been postponing telling the news to Malcolm because I wanted to do it face to face and not over the telephone. In truth, I was dreading the moment. I was in love and still hoped to marry him in the future despite the set-back. I had been his constant companion for months now and our love strengthened every day.

Circumstances had changed the tide. Now that I was out of the government, I had to leave the country whether I liked it or not. I had to fulfill my commitment with Radio Australia. For once, I had no control of my own destiny, but let myself carried away by a mysterious force. And this time, it was not my doing.

Malcolm was still married, and who knew how long we had to wait for his wife to consent to divorce. This opportunity was bestowed on me as if it were predestined. To accept it or not was no longer my choice. I could not help being excited and thrilled with the prospect of a new adventure.

Actually working for a news organization had been beyond my dreams and hopes. Escaping Viet Nam and its narrow minded society meant a lot to me. I had never belonged to the country heart and soul. I always considered myself an outsider. How did I succeed in accomplishing these two important wishes without raising a finger! I kept repeating this in my sleep and in my wakeful days. I was in the land of the Wizard of Oz. I was high above the cloud, all the clichés to describe my state of mind. Would Malcolm understand this?

The next day Malcolm called and we agreed to go out for dinner after work. We went to a noodle soup restaurant near Malcolm's office and home.

"Were you very busy yesterday?"

"Yes," I answered softly, my eyes glued to the noodle soup, searching for a way to announce the news.

"I was out in Bien Hoa, interviewing an American captain. It was mildly interesting," Malcolm said.

"I just resigned from the Ministry," I looked up at him.

"Any problem?... You got the job with ABC?" He almost shouted aloud. "Oh! Baby!" He reached out for my hand, his eyes clouded. He slid his fingers between mine and squeezed them again and again.

"When did you know?"

"Actually, I didn't. Mr. Hieu called me into his office to inform me and signed for my release." I told him the whole event.

He sadly smiled and released my hand to light up a cigarette. We remained silent. He called for the check and we walked back home in silence. Once inside the apartment, he wrapped his arms around me and held me tight, smothering me in his chest while resting his head on the top of mine.

"Oh Baby, I love you so much!" We held our embrace for a long time in the dark. I was choked with emotion and on the verge of tears. Still holding me, he slowly steered me towards the bed and laid me down. We kissed and clung to one another. I stayed with him that night.

Malcolm was tender and loving. No reproach, no blame came out of his mouth. But he was devastated. I also realized that I had never loved anyone as I loved Malcolm. I kept asking myself whether I had done the right thing by sacrificing my love for a career. I might never find someone who loved me as much as Malcolm did. It was too late. I could not resign my post and stay in Saigon.

"I promise you that I'll win the divorce. I'll not give you up. I love you too much. I can wait."

"Yes darling. I can also wait and we will be together somehow." I strongly believed him.

A week later, I went to the meeting. All five chosen candidates, two females and three males, ranging from 28 (I was the youngest) to 45, were introduced to the ABC executive director who came to Saigon for this special event. He welcomed us and gave a short speech about the organization and the new project.

The schedule for us to leave Saigon was in mid September. There would be a stop in Singapore for two days to visit the ABC "Voice of Australia" staff, and then we would continue on to Sidney. That left me one and a half months to get ready. The most troublesome task was to secure a passport and exit visa. As I had mentioned before, bureaucracy and corruption went hand in hand. I had plenty of time to apply and wait. I knew that I had the Australian Embassy's backing and therefore I refused to pay bribes. I spent hours going back and forth to that office for several days – another example to reinforce my will to leave.

I spent as much time as I could with Malcolm. He was also very busy. The Kennedy Administration had decided to build up the Vietnamese Armed Forces. Advisors and military Special Forces personnel were sent to train the Vietnamese. Being bureau chief of the Associated Press (AP), Malcolm had a staff consisting of a Vietnamese assistant reporter, an office clerk, and a freelance photographer. There was no computer or internet at that period, all news was typed and sent by mail or telegraph through the Post Office. Working for a wire service meant filing reports day and night, however trivial or important the news was.

Malcolm's fear of being beaten by his competitor, the United Press International (UPI), kept him on guard 24/7. So he was under tremendous pressure, and our meetings were spaced out. Between medical visits, shots against various tropical deceases and packing, and saying goodbye to relatives and friends, I barely had time to relax. Malcolm and I had never been to Australia before; we hardly brought up the subject of my trip during the rest of my remaining time in Saigon. Malcolm took it very hard, although on the surface he was cool. Fortunately, his job helped distract him.

As for me, I lived in "virtual reality" – that was of course unknown at that time. Some days, I lived in a state of uncontrollable exuberance and high spirits. I walked around with my chin up – I was employed by the prestigious Radio Australia, and soon, these Vietnamese would hear my voice through "The Voice of Australia."

Other times, I was filled with anxiety and loneliness. In desperation, I kept telling myself to be courageous, to stand up firmly, and to thank my stars for a new future.

The inevitable departure approaching, I decided to skip the Singapore stop, thus giving me two extra days to spend with Malcolm. I would take an Air France direct flight to Sidney to join the team there.

The flight was scheduled for 6 p.m. A black hole seemed to swallow my memory of that day. All I could remember was that my whole family and Malcolm accompanied me to the airport. At that time, the Tan Son Nhat air terminal was nothing bigger than a one-story mansion. The ground floor was for ticket and luggage check-in, while an open terrace on top permitted friends and families to watch passengers leaving or arriving. (In 2016, Saigon airport had become as fashionable and up to date as any European airport, with fancy stores and several international restaurants.)

At the time, though, the runway was so short it could only accommodate propeller airplanes like the Constellation and small aircraft. The Boeing 707 jetliner was not admitted until a year or two later. Once I checked in, I went up to the top terrace to join my family and Malcolm. The loudspeaker announced the boarding gate number, and I looked at Malcolm, tears running down my cheeks. I embraced every member of my family. Malcolm took me in his arms, and I buried my face in his chest. No words came from any of us. I ran down the staircase and blindly staggered my way to the plane.

(Note: Unexpectedly, I realize that remembering this painful time has affected my writing. It is as if it were yesterday. Memories of our love, our happiness, our youth surged within me, Malcolm's young smiling face fading in and out of my eyes. The depression and loneliness that have been buried inside me for the last four years, since Malcolm's death, suddenly gave rise to uncontrolled emotion. For three days I could not bring myself to write.)

The sky got dark as the airplane taxied along the runway. I looked through my tears and through the curtained window as the plane began to roar upward. Images of blurred human hands waving zoomed by as fast as a bullet, and then the darkly lit panorama of Saigon appeared below. For no reason, I recalled my sad trip home from Paris and how much I had hated to leave that beautiful city to go back to a bleak Viet Nam. And here I was, flying away from it in such a state that I began to curse my own fate.

Foreign correspondents attending a military briefing.

Accompanying foreign correspondents to a plantation.

A gala dinner with staff of Viet Nam Press and colleagues.

Malcolm and I at his Saigon apartment.

CHAPTER FIVE

I looked out hoping to catch a final view of Saigon. But the plane was already out over the sea. It was a dark night with a few flickering lights of fishing boats below. The sky was scintillating with stars like diamonds on a black background. I had always been attracted to this kind of sky where stars looked down on me, shining and hypnotizing. The moonless sky displayed its magical world, begging me to join it, its multiple stars mischievously blinking and consorting with me. "You are too romantic and sentimental," I thought. I longingly stared at the sky, wishing to be one of these tiny twinkling stars.

I sat back, and let the humming of the plane lull me to slumber. I somberly reviewed the events of the day. Between confusion and emotions, I hardly remembered much of what had been said or done these past several hours. I was still in shock, ruminating through all the past events that finally led me to the present time. Almost two years had gone by, with so many changes within a short time.

Somehow my thoughts gradually drifted off to the time I stepped down the Air France ramp to enter Tan Son Nhat airport back at the end of 1959. I had no notion at the time what my future would be. I had brushed away the dismal thought that there was no return and entered the terminal. I immediately felt like "Alice In Wonderland," with my distinctive appearance in Western dress while all the women around, including my mother and sister, were in their "ao dai." Like Alice, I must have looked weird and diminutive in that "Rabbit Hole." It was another world, and not the same one that I had left a decade before. I didn't recognize anything, and the sun was so bright, I was suffocating and intimidated among my own people. I was paralyzed with emotions and hopelessly lost.

I had not a cent on me, and I had to depend on my mother's meager salary until I settled down with a job. At least, I had a job waiting for me. Beyond that, I had never questioned whether or not I would be happy living in a void all my life. I had blocked my mind from making any plan or having any ambitious illusions of avoiding disappointment and depression. Being a woman fresh out of college with little experience in life, and especially in my native country, I was doomed in advance to a monotonous and compliant existence.

"Live and let live," I had made up my mind to do that. "Follow the crowd," or more accurately "follow the wind." I had skipped "Follow your instinct." For fear of repeating myself, for the last two years, before my departure for Australia, I had lived a daydreaming life, surrendering control of my own fate to chance. Naivety and uncertainty in the beginning had slowly begun to open up to hope and contentment. I had gained self-confidence, success, and love. So why did I throw it all away? For what? Pursuit of adventure? Another caprice or just pure self-promotion?

"Nonsense, the truth was elusive," I decided. "Luck and self-preservation both played a big parallel role here." Despite my pretention of letting go, I had learned through mistakes and struggles to gain a foothold for my life. It was a gradual learning process I had enforced upon myself, a young wide-eyed girl becoming a more mature woman with a will to survive. I, along with an invisible helping hand, had carved a life for myself. My separation from Malcolm was intentional, despite my attribution of it to circumstances. My relationship with him could not get anywhere without his wife's consent for divorce. I began to feel guilty for having illicit love affairs. I never did doubt Malcolm's love for me, but I also had my pride and reputation, being an official in a society full of contradictions and controversies.

Among friends and social acquaintances, we were known as steady couple. Nevertheless, two threats had constantly been looming over me. Malcolm's wife now had me as her rival and could concoct tales that could harm me if I were still a civil servant. Or I might be accused of collaborating with the foreign press, if ever Malcolm wrote something that displeased the regime. One AP journalist had been deported before I came to work at the Ministry. Foreign correspondents were never safe in an authoritarian regime.

My perception proved to be correct. One month after I left for Australia, I was informed by Malcolm that Jim Robinson, an NBC reporter, had been expelled from Viet Nam despite the intervention of the American Ambassador and the president of the company. François Sully, a French freelance reporter for Newsweek, who had lived in Viet Nam for decades, was also expelled. During the Buddhist upheaval in 1963, many other foreign reporters were either detained, threatened or expelled. Eventually, in 1972, Malcolm, too, was banned from Viet Nam for several years.

So when I had learned about the possibility of working for the "Voice of Australia," I was desperate to go, but realistically I knew it would be hopeless unless I had outside help. That was the reason why I had not bothered to apply earlier. It was a gift from heaven, or predestined fate, when I ran into my Australian friend who gave me that chance -- a chance to turn over a new leaf, so to speak. My future from now on was secure, and not in Viet Nam. The aero-dynamic force of will, along with the outside influence, had mysteriously conspired to let me realize my hidden aspiration.

Sadly, my luck had not made provision for love. After grief and sorrows in my love life, I had found love and happiness with Malcolm, but now, here I was, separated from him by thousands of miles.

Is there some proverb somewhere that says: "Lucky in cards, unlucky in love?" May be that was my destiny: to remain a spinster after all. Being alone again, and going to a free democratic country like Australia, I had a chance to test my resilience against defeat. Was it wise for me to run away from happiness? Or was it, again, mistrust -- of Malcolm, and men in general? Analyses and arguments kept colliding in my head as the plane flew farther and farther from my past.

The plane landed in Darwin in pitch-dark night around 2 a.m. I stepped out of the plane and a hot gust of air slapped my face. "What? Is Australia that hot?" It took me by surprise. I followed other passengers to a shack for the two-hour layover. Everything was eerily quiet except for the buzzing of mosquitoes in my ears. I vividly imagined myself sitting in the dark somewhere in the jungle of the Viet Nam Delta. I was exhausted and drained of emotion.

By the time the plane approached Sydney, I looked down and recognized that famous bridge below. I felt some excitement mounting in me. It had been arranged for the Vietnamese team to meet me at the terminal.

"Welcome to Sydney!" exclaimed the director of Radio Australia, my new boss, whose name I have forgotten. "I hope that you are not too tired to spend some time with us."

Bleary with sleep and mentally unprepared for the reception, I vaguely remember the director of the "Voice of Australia" taking us to the ABC headquarters and showing us around the working place to introduce us to various editors. Later we toured the city and dined with the big boss. All this happened in a haze, and even now I cannot remember any particular details.

The next day we flew to Melbourne, where our jobs and future home were waiting for us. The home was a two-storied villa with five furnished bedrooms, but it was in a desolate neighborhood outside Melbourne, some 25 minutes by rail from the city. The front yard was unkempt with brown grass and bare of any other vegetation. It was September, spring season in the Southern hemisphere. And yet the sight filled me with melancholy and desolation.

"We had a hard time finding a suitable house for you," the assistant said. "I hope you like it." Shared living arrangements in what I thought was a dismal place.

The rest of the team, especially the men, were glowing over the house -- they had never lived abroad before. "It looks fine," Hung, a designated head of our team, enthusiastically answered. "We will work it out among ourselves."

Having lived in France and England for many years, I snobbishly looked upon suburbanites as little bourgeois. In addition, I had never lived with strangers before in my life. And here we were, two men and two women, to live in that house. And a third man was supposed to join us later. We had agreed to consult among ourselves before making any decisions concerning our co-habitation. The two women on the team were to have their bedrooms on the ground floor, and the men would be on the second floor. We were supposed to discuss the sharing of our domicile in a "democratic spirit." But Minh, my female colleague, was quick to grab the back bedroom, leaving me with the front one, where she and anyone who wanted to visit her had to cross my bedroom before entering hers. I began to feel uncomfortable. I hardly knew these people.

I promised myself that I would find a room in town later on.

We were left free that day to unpack and settle down. The next day, we were fetched by one of the director's assistants to visit different international departments of the "Voice of Australia." We were introduced to the staffs from South East Asia, Thailand, Indonesia, Philippines, Japan, and China.

At the Thai and Indonesian departments, I was amused to be singled out as a "datable" woman for bachelors in the future. "Here is somebody single for you to go out with," a Thai woman nodded to one of her colleagues. I smiled and nodded back.

"You seem destined to be a flower girl," Minh told me after we were alone.

"What do you mean, 'flower girl?'" I felt a bit insulted.

"What I mean is that you are attractive," she lied.

That afternoon, we started our on-the-job training. Each of us was tested for voice and reading ability. I had the premonition that whatever my voice was, I was already assigned to administrative work. My voice was too soft, and also they preferred a Northern accent that was more musical and warm for radio broadcasting. After two weeks of training, we were given a permanent office on the ground floor of the ABC building. Thus the new "Voice of Australia" in Vietnamese began.

Our schedule was from 1 p.m. to 9 p.m., with an hour for lunch. The first broadcast was scheduled at 7. I thought of my family and Malcolm glued to the shortwave radio that day whatever the local time was.

As soon as I had the new address, I immediately sent mail to Malcolm and my family. It took a week to reach them in those days. Meantime, I began to settle down to work, consisting of translating into Vietnamese all the news for the nightly broadcast sent to us from the news room above us. I also kept the ledger as well as the staff timetable.

Each day, we left home at 11:45 a.m. for the train station, which was walking distance from our home. The train arrived at 12 and pulled into Melbourne station around 12:25 or later. Every morning, we set out with attaché cases in hand, trooping to the station, men in front, followed by the women.

"We are four Musketeers," I laughed aloud. "Off we go to work."

My co-workers just smiled, obviously not amused. Truly, we seemed to be attached by an invisible umbilical cord. We were housed together, shopped together, shared meals together, took transportation together and worked together. In other words we lived like couples 24 hours a day. We were dutifully assigned specific household tasks. Each of us had his or her own room to clean, and the men could do some vacuum cleaning in the hall. For dinner, women cooked and men washed the dishes. Not knowing their taste, at first, I cooked the easiest and most popular Vietnamese dish, fried chicken on ginger with vegetables and, of course, rice. I did not remember what Minh cooked. I was so upset at each meal that I hardly paid attention to what I ate.

Hieu was the cause of my mental agony. Tall and middle-aged, Hieu came from central Viet Nam. He was a poet and a reclusive philosopher. Thin, with dark, unhealthy skin and a lot of short black hair, he was tall for a Vietnamese man. He was always moody and aloof. I did not know anything about his life in Viet Nam, whether or not he was married, or whether he had a family -- I never heard him speaking of one. His manner and attitude were those of a Vietnamese man who had never been outside of his own circle, and, most of all, lacked sophistication and appropriate social behavior.

That, by itself, never bothered me as long as we observed social distance. But at the table, it was a different matter. In the middle of every meal, Hieu would start to cough and loudly gurgle, with mucus in his throat. At the end, he spat out the disgusting stuff into a pot next to him. Each time he did it, I would suddenly lose my appetite. My stomach churned, and it took great self-control to keep from getting sick. The others at the table silently continued to eat as if nothing had occurred. Several times I was so nauseated and disgusted that I had to control myself before I spat out words I would regret later. So at every meal, I rushed to finish eating before his indigestion began. I was not always successful.

I had been expecting someone to say something about his bad habit, but no one else seemed to be disturbed by it. It could be that Hieu was the oldest of the group, and, according to the Vietnamese culture, one had to respect the elderly by not offending. I dreaded dinner every evening and left the table more and more often in despair. Two weeks after our arrival, I gathered my courage and announced that I would no longer share the meals with them. I didn't have the courage to tell the truth but gave some obscure reason. I avoided blaming Hieu so not to cause any discord.

"If you don't like what we cook," Minh looked disturbed, "you can always cook your own and share with us."

"No, I always eat too fast," I turned red with embarrassment. "And besides, I am tired after work and prefer to go to bed early."

"As you like." The team ended the meal in silence. I sighed with relief. I kept telling myself that I had to find a room in town. Somehow, though, I never found time to look.

Two weeks after we were settled in, I received an invitation from the Indonesian section for a Saturday evening outing. I was overjoyed to be able to get away. A car came to pick me up at home. Inside, I had to squeeze in next to two Indonesian men sitting at the back. They were young and loud. We were three females and three males packed in a small car. Being new in town, I had no notion of where we went. At some point, the car stopped at an isolated place. It was pitch dark with a few shimmering street lights far off. I stepped out, followed by my date. I saw the girl in front get out and rush towards our open door to get in beside the man in the back seat. "What fun!" she shouted.

My date and I stood next to the car, not knowing what to do. Soon, to my horror, the two couples in the dark, closed car began copulating, kissing and moaning while I and my supposed boyfriend were left to our own devices outside. Embarrassed and wordless, we looked at each other and awkwardly smiled.

Indonesians were Asians, I thought, and Asian girls of all types were supposed to be reserved and discreet in public. The most allowable physical display was holding hands in the street. Even bar girls and prostitutes in Vietnam never publicly exposed their affections by such indecent behavior. It was such a shocking display that I promised myself that I would never accept their invitation again. But it was the only one they made.

Being new in town, and busy during week days, I did my best to keep cool and I promised myself to find a way to make friends outside my social circle. Before I left Viet Nam, two women from the "Moral Rearmament" movement had been coming to my office to ask for assistance to set up a political play called "The Year of the Tiger." (Moral Rearmament was an international politico-religious society that was against war and violence, but beyond that I was not clear about their cause.) The political play was about riots and demonstrations that took place in Japan in 1950s. Diem saw the play as part of education for his military officers to learn how to cope with disturbances.

When the MR women had learned that I was going to Australia to work, they brought some letters and asked me to deliver them by hand to their group in Melbourne. "I am sure that my friends in Melbourne would love to meet you," one lady said.

So I executed their orders two weeks after my arrival by calling them up. The members were so pleased that they invited me for lunch and I became their friend. Whenever there was some public event such as a picnic organized by their group, or a demonstration to support the aboriginals, the native tribes of Australia, I was invited to join them. These events of course carried some political messages against the establishment. I suspected that they were trying to convert me to their cause.

"I hope you like Melbourne," one of the women told me one day. "I know that it might take time to get used to living here, but you always have us."

They were kind and friendly to me and it was my only opportunity to mingle with the Australian community. I rarely had any other occasion to meet other Australians, including those with whom we shared offices. Racial discrimination was still evident at that time. I was aware that few pedestrians or store keepers gave us friendly greetings as we walked by. I never had a glimpse of our neighbors throughout our stay in that house, not even on weekends.

A few days after my first date with the Indonesians, a Thai man called to invite me out for a Saturday evening. I again accepted with some misgiving. At least, I had met him and he looked like a nice decent man. (Unfortunately, his name was long and difficult to pronounce, and I confess that I cannot remember it. For the purpose of identification, I will call him Thai.)

He was a little over five feet tall, compact, with a slow manner and soft of speech. He lived alone and had worked for Radio Australia for more than a year. My first date with him was pleasant, friendly and correct. He was in his early 30s, his short haircut made his face more square than oval. I had no problem identifying him as a Thai because of his dark skin, big eyes and reserved manner. Thai and I got along right away.

We agreed to go out every Saturday and sometimes Sunday, whenever I felt free. He had a car to take me anywhere I wanted to go. We went to the zoo to see these animals -- cute Koala bears, tamed Kangaroos, giant ostriches that we could ride, Tasmanian Devils, and other exotic beasts. We dined at different restaurants and leisurely visited different bars. We travelled to the seaside, to the desert, to public parks. We even were caught in a sandstorm one day. Melbourne was bordered by sand desert and we were warned that September was the worst month for a sandstorm. I had seen movies of them and was aroused by curiosity to be in or near one. Melbourne was a big town of some 500,000 inhabitants, with high-rise buildings in the center and small shaded villas in outlying sections, but that day, Radio Australia was warning inhabitants every few minutes to stay indoors if they had no business outside.

"I have never seen a sandstorm in my life," I said to Thai. "Would you mind if we drive somewhere safe enough to watch it?" Thai looked at me, amused and mischievous.

"Why not, I know some place safe enough, if the storm is not strong." I was thrilled. So we jumped into the car and drove off.

The sky was as brown as the sand. The streets were empty of pedestrians and all windows were shut. An eerie silence reigned everywhere. The town was under siege. We drove to the edge of the desert, a sharp divide between the town and the flat sandy territory. We stepped out, watching the brown cloud swirling and scooping sand and dust in the distance. Suddenly a gust slapped sand on our face. I felt pain on my cheeks and sand in my eyes and mouth. My clothing was covered with sand. We rushed to the car and sat there watching the wrath of the storm. It was frightening, and yet it was the most elating experience I ever encountered.

On the whole I was so grateful to have someone with whom to share it. One evening, Thai invited me to dine at his sister's home. I was a bit leery because, up to then, we were just friends. Thai knew that I was engaged to Malcolm. Most of our conversations during our outings were more about the country, our activities in the office or the beautiful places we had visited or planned to visit. We never touched on our personal lives out of respect for privacy.

"Would it be a nuisance for your sister to cook?" I shyly asked.

"She wanted to meet you and she loves to cook anyway," Thai calmly answered. "She is good at cooking Thai dishes."

I loved Thai cuisine, which is similar to Vietnamese, and there were no Thai or Vietnamese restaurants in the area at that time. We sometimes ate at Chinese restaurants, which were considered exotic and were therefore pricy.

Being invited to dinner and to meet his folks was an honor and a privilege reserved to more intimate friends. Thai's young and attractive sister received us in her house, a small villa in some area unfamiliar to me. The inside was tastefully decorated with Thai artifacts and paintings. The living room also served as the dining room. The dining table was already neatly laid with rice bowls and chopsticks.

At the age of 30, his sister wore Western dress, and her long black hair was combed back into a chignon, exposing her delicate facial features. She was warm and gracious, a trait of a well-educated person. She received us alone; I don't remember whether she was married with family or not. It was normal in Asia that the family was not required to be present if the guest was a friend of one member of the family but not of the others. Or maybe Thai's sister, by curiosity, discreetly wanted to meet me, and tell her brother what she thought.

Our table conversation was more or less about Melbourne and vicinity. I felt at home and enjoyed the meal. Thai was my opposite: he was calm and reserved while I was always ebullient with curiosity and sensitive and emotional if being challenged. I was gratified to have met another good friend so soon to alleviate my frustration at being away from Malcolm and my family, all of whom I sadly missed.

By now, I had eased into a daily routine, getting up in the morning, preparing breakfast and dinner for the evening, cleaning house and doing laundry on weekends. We always got home around 10 p.m., enough time to heat up dinner and prepare for bed. If the weather turned bad on some Sundays, I took the opportunity to catch up with my personal business and answering my mail.

Two weeks after I arrived in Melbourne, I received letters from my mother, my sister and of course Malcolm. I read my family's mail first, in which my mother described the scene after my departure.

"I have never seen any man who wept openly after you left," my mother wrote, accusing me of being cruel-hearted to have left Malcolm. My heart started beating wildly and my hands shook violently when I tried to open Malcolm's letters. He wrote every day after I left, five of them he had stuffed together into a manila envelope while waiting for my new address so he could send them. As I opened the package, I caught his hand-writing on the first envelope. Tears were running down my face (and even now I am choked with emotion) as I read what it said: "Read this on the plane before you go to sleep."

Inside the letter Malcolm dated it: "20 minutes after leaving your house, Monday Sept 17, 1962."

My dearest-
We have just said good night for the last time in a while. As you read thi. you are high in the sky. Perhaps fishermen on some ocean-going boat car. hear a rumble in the sky as you streak among the stars."

It was three pages, typewritten, itemizing all the anxieties that I myself have described when I was on the plane that night. I was struck by his perception of my inner soul and by the accuracies of his interpretation of my thoughts, as if a sudden current of telepathy had crossed between us. Our thoughts had commingled in the middle of the South China Sea that very night. He spelled out, one by one, all my anguishes of uncertainty, of suspicion, of separation, of faith in him and of our ever meeting again.

He then concluded: "But my darling, there is a spark left that is more than a memory. It is our love, and it will return, if we nurse it and fan it and keep it glowing brightly.

We could have said adieu forever tonight. We didn't. This is the first step. Let us take the rest, one by one, until we have conquered this enemy of separation and danger.

Good night, my darling. Sleep soundly and be strong. I shall be solid as a rock in my love for you."

I cried and cried and wished that I could go back and lie next to him, my face against his. I never had such a love letter, and it tore my heart and limbs. He spoke of my tortuous soul and of my deep anguish of self-doubt. I spent the rest of the day sulky and miserable. (My present state of mind, after rereading this letter, plunges me into despair and loneliness. I feel him close to me and visualize his young handsome face, a face that I loved and cherished for over 50 years. I feel a physical pain all over and weirdly imagine myself being 28 again, waiting for him to come back from a military operation. He is still haunting me after his death in August of 2012.)

I counted over 60 letters and 5 cables that Malcolm wrote within three months – 5 letters a week. They were three pages long and painfully described his love for me and our future, how he was going to take care of me once we got married. He also talked of his work and the situation in Viet Nam. Being a good writer and a reporter, he filled me in with everyday activities he was going through covering the war, traveling to different parts of the country, being shot at and witnessing killing on both sides, observing and even escaping American helicopter crashes and reporting American casualties. Some of his writings were contemplative and heart rendering. He faithfully wrote me in his spare time, during office work or late at night.

On my twenty-eighth birthday, I received a box of 12 long-stem dark roses along with a little booklet he had hand-illustrated that began: "Saturday, Nov. 10, 1962: the world is in a sad state of affairs.(AP)

It all began when a brilliant, little girl got a bright, bad, little idea... from a smooth-talking rat at a cocktail party. So she got on a big, ugly airplane and flew away..." It ended with a drawing of a red broken heart with our initiatives. Malcolm was romantic after all. It was the first time I had been presented with his inner feelings.

"Happy Birthday," Minh said, seeing the bouquet. "He must have loved you so much to write you every day."

"Yes, and I am miserable because I miss him so much," I answered angrily, as if she had challenged me and my sincerity.

"Time will heal," Minh said as I stared at her with hostility. I stayed silent.

I just visualized Malcolm sitting at his empty dining table drawing these cute figures of me and him and the rat and attaching photos of him and the Koala Bear. I took a rose stem, put the booklet near my heart, and went out to celebrate my birthday with my friend, Thai.

Thai looked at the rose stem and stayed silent. I was grateful that he didn't pester me with questions. He just proposed to take me to a bar for the occasion. I had written to Malcolm about Thai and how happy I was to have a good friend to ease my boredom. I received a three-page letter warning me of Thai's motives, warning me that sooner or later Thai would end up falling in love with me. I was not worried because Thai knew my love for Malcolm was strong and durable.

Another time, Malcolm sent me an urgent short letter in which he claimed that someone had opened our mail, and, to counterattack, he had included a small plastic bag with a folded paper marked in big red letters with the word "SECRET." I took out the little note inside and read:

To: Mail Censor
PosteTelegraphe Telephone
Saigon
Sir: The note you are now reading has been treated with especially prepared bacterial toxins.
\Touching it has contaminated your hand sufficiently that within 24 hours you can expect to become seriously ill. The

disease is not fatal, but it is discomfort for a period of about three weeks.
The opening or tampering with mail is against the laws of the Republic of Viet Nam. This will serve as a reminder to you of the desirability of nonconforming with these laws.

Sincerely, MWB"

I was puzzled and amused at the same time, figuring that it was a genial joke. Malcolm was ahead of his time. Such a trick has turned out to be occasionally used, nowadays, as an assassination weapon against political opponents, in particular against Russian activists. Malcolm was far ahead of this subversive method of threats before anything like this started happening twenty years later. Regarding the strict censorship in Viet Nam, Malcolm suspected that his letters might be opened. He knew he might be under surveillance for what he wrote about the war and the American intervention that might have upset the government.

In later letters, Malcolm did mention his interviews with the CIA and with American Ambassador. In one letter, he talked of James Robinson of NBC being expelled and the foreign press giving a farewell party for him after failing to get the government to change its mind. And Mme Nhu, the powerful acting "first lady," had surprised them by attending the party, flirting with the foreign correspondents and declaring how much she honored freedom of speech. Then she left a propaganda pamphlet denouncing the foreign press.

Malcolm's letters kept me going. They were full of wit and information from home. He bared his soul and his sensitivity to humanity in these letters. For example, in one of my letters to him, I had casually mentioned a hobby store that I accidently discovered in Melbourne and how sorry I was for having broken the landing gear on his model plane.

I was struck by his emotional response: "It is more fun for adults to shop for toys, but I can't help remembering that when I was a boy, I counted it very lucky to get a present of a model airplane kit. These cost 10 cents (maybe 12 piastres at the current rate} and consisted of little more than plans, balsa wood, and silk paper. With a week or so of painstaking work, a boy could build one of these things into a fragile but very beautiful model airplane that would fly beautifully. I loved them – and I think I loved them especially because they were so difficult to make. As I grew older, I used to buy my own wood and parts, and design my own planes. In building them, I learned many interesting and surprising things about the science of aerodynamics. Seemingly perfect designs wouldn't fly at all sometimes, and it took many days figuring out why not. And when I discovered what it was, and when I had something that would fly with grace and beauty, I was proud and happy. In younger years, I always wanted to be an aeronautical engineer – one who designs airplanes. I got interested in other things as I grew older, and look what I am doing now. But flight in all its forms has always been very dear to my heart…But to this day, when I am near an airplane, particularly a small one like the light planes used for artillery spotting, something in me feels very warm and fine; somehow these little planes are as familiar to me as my own body. I know every hinge and pin in them, and the beautiful but subtle simplicity that makes them fly. And you know, it is a terrible thing to say, but to me, a woman is something like one of these airplanes I used to love. Somehow there is a sensuous similarity between a perfectly designed airplane and a perfectly designed woman… I can't exactly explain what I do mean, because I don't exactly understand it myself."

And I broke the landing gear of his kit! Being apart, we seemed to be more open and frank with each other. We became more intimate and learned more about each other without feeling embarrassed or hurting one other. Malcolm's letters exposed deep feelings for his country, his love for humanity and its fragility. It was for the first time that I truly discovered his moral values and his personal feelings. One letter touched me profoundly. In it, he wrote:

"…I am going to write a long, rambling story about the 57th helicopter company, the first American fighting unit to come here.

I mean this story to be a kind of eulogy to the men and machines who have stood up under nearly a year of exhaustion, fear, danger, boredom and all the other things that company has gone through. I've flown with them many times since they arrived last December, but only today was I somehow struck by what has happened to them at this time. Out of the 24 helicopters they had originally, all but five are now broken down, shot down or otherwise incapacitated. The five that are still flying are a mass of patches over the bullet holes, the paint is a mess where different tones of olive drab have been used to cover scars, there are blood stains on the floors of some of them, most the windows are smashed out. They have had a lot of casualties of their own. Last week, a young machine gunner on one was torn to pieces by 12 bullets from a Viet Cong tommy gun. During the occasional days off the men have, they sit around the 'lounge' next to the operations shack, a small room where there is a magazine rack, a ping-pong table and some chairs. At night they sometimes go to Saigon for a few beers at one of the dismal bars and come home early, because there's usually an operation first thing in the morning. And they go to bed in stifling, mosquito-infested tents, brave Americans, and everything nasty I often say about Americans does not apply to them."

I did not have the occasion to read the article, nor was I aware whether or not he wrote it with the same feelings he had expressed in his letter to me. The irony was that Viet Nam war was not very popular with the Americans in the USA and anyone living at that period knew how poorly Viet Nam veterans were treated once they returned home. I was proud of Malcolm, but it made me anxious to think about being reunited with him. Being pessimistic on the whole, I always carried a gloomy thought of being a magnet for disasters. I constantly lived in fear of losing my loved ones and of losing Malcolm in one of these horrible operations.

I learned more about Malcolm's feelings and character in these letters than I could have possibly learned living with him for decades. I am glad that I have reserved these precious letters, which represented a golden period when people still wrote letters to one another. In one of my letters to him (unfortunately, I did not find any of my letters to him in his archives), I must have discussed the relationship between the Vietnamese people and the Americans. It provoked a passionate patriotic response from Malcolm that I had never known before.

"I know Vietnamese people don't trust us. I think it is mainly because they don't know us. Up until a very few years ago, the only big noses they knew were Europeans. I think every Vietnamese basically thinks of Americans as Europeans, call themselves whatever they want. But we are not Europeans. Our whole way of looking at life is completely different from that of any country in Europe, including England and the Commonwealth countries. I don't say we are better or worse – there are points on both sides – but just different.

I enclose something from Viet Nam press – (in which Mr. Tuyen, the head of the Tu Do publishing house, said: Americans are hard-working people, fundamentally democratic-minded, who fight hard to preserve their freedom as individuals and as a nation.) I know it's propaganda, but at the same time, it is the most sincerely nice thing I have ever seen written about America by a Vietnamese. It is easy to say nice things about any country if one is doing it purely for propaganda, but somehow if this Pham Viet Tuyen really feels as he does, I am very pleased because it somehow sounds a very warm chord in me. Any American likes to think of his country exactly as Tuyen describes it. Personally, I think he is absolutely right. You know perfectly well that I can be strongly anti-American, too, and I can bring up reasons for being nti-American far better than any you could think of, because I know my eople. But please don't judge us too harshly yourself until you know us – ot just the handful of correspondents and other miscellaneous bums you ave met. Remember that Europeans don't trust us either, or else assume we re naïve fools. But at the same time, if the people who call us the worst names vould look at our history, they would see we have done pretty well. We have nore personal freedom in the U.S. than any other nation except some of the Commonwealth countries and Denmark. And at the same time, despite the tupidity we show sometimes, we have managed to keep the free world free for long time, in two world wars and a number of small ones. Could any Euro-ean or Asian nation say that much? We have never had or wanted colonies except perhaps the Philippines, which we turned loose as soon as they were leveloped,) and being a former colony ourselves, we have always given at least ome kind of support to most new, small countries – not just to stop commu-ism or for political reasons, but because Americans don't believe in pushing mall countries around.

All right, I have now exposed you to a half page of American propa-ganda. It serves you right, my darling, for all the Vietnamese propaganda you nade me read when you were with the DGI (department of Information.) So iow we'll go live in Kabul."

Who could have any time to sit down these days to passionately and incerely write such a long patriotic essay as this? Another time, I was very roud of him for some story that he only revealed to me, and, as a consci-ntious correspondent, he would not report before consulting first with an American commander. I called that self-censorship and responsible. He wrote: "By the way, here is the piece of news I hope you'll keep to yourself for the time eing; it's too hot even for me to do anything about for the moment. If I were o use it it would seriously endanger a number of people, who certainly would e court-martialed immediately. But just for your benefit, here it is: There now re several squadrons of the latest American jet fighters, flown by Americans, in Viet Nam. They are flying most of the time at night, so they won't be noticed y characters like me. One of the things they do is fly faster than the speed of ound, which is a weapon in itself. When a plane flies faster than sounds, it reates something called sonic boom. On the ground, this sounds like a deafen-ng explosion. It breaks glass, shakes buildings badly, and can injure people. It's oretty bad when the airplane is 10,000 feet high. You can imagine what it's like when the plane is only 500 feet high. And that's what they're doing over places ike D-Zone – at 2 in the morning. They also patrol the S.Vietnamese borders

looking for enemy planes. I learn that Russian planes have been supplied t
the VC. The U.S. jets already have shot one of these down, it seems, and th
wrecked plane is believed to have disintegrated in the jungle below.

So you can see, I have a hot story. The only trouble with it is that I ha-
ven't figured out what to do with it yet. I am going to talk to a general I know
tomorrow to try to persuade him to shake some of it loose." (I cannot help bu
keep thinking what Malcolm would think about the present political turmoil
I went to watch a documentary film "Dateline: Saigon, "about the five young
'Turks', as they were called at that time, the war correspondents Peter Arnett
Malcolm, Neil Sheehan, David Halberstam and Horst Faas in the early '60s
After the show, a panel that included the head of the Committee to Protect
Journalists, a reporter from the Politico Publishing and someone else. One
panelist viewed the journalists as naïve. I figured that not too many people
in the audience had lived during the '60s so as to grasp the danger that these
young journalists faced and the courage they needed to get them through it.

Despite the censorship imposed on the foreign press by the Diem regime, it was lenient, because the Vietnamese officials did not understand the
subtlety of the English language. As for the Americans, no US president up
until Trump ever considered the press as enemy of the people. So for me, there
is a big gap between the way the press covered the war in Viet Nam and the
way the war in Middle East is covered. Soon, the Viet Nam war will fade away
and become just part of history.)

Every time I got one of Malcolm's letters, there was always some interesting news or new problems he faced. I found in this one the most horrific
story involving a reporter that I ever heard.

It happened this way (not that it will be of much interest to you, but
I tell you anyway;) Perry, Halberstam (of the NY Times) and I were out, all
on separate helicopters. We left Can Tho for a group of VC hamlets about 50
km to the east, roughly half way between Can Tho and Tra Vinh. I was in the
No.4 helicopter, Perry on No.5, and Halberstam in No.6. You know how these
things go; when you're still about 10km from the objective, the helicopters
always drop down to about one meter from the ground, flying at top speed. It's
a little dangerous, but it surprises the VC, because they can't see or hear you
coming from very far away, and it's actually the safest way, because they don't
have time to shoot accurately. Well, we landed next to the hamlet, drawing
moderately heavy enemy machinegun fire. Not accurate, though. We could see
the bullets hitting the rice paddy water at least 50 meters away. But anyway,
helicopters like to land their troops as quickly as possible, especially when they

are under fire, because a helicopter is most vulnerable when it's on the ground.

The troops normally unload very fast, and the helicopter is almost never on the ground more than 6 seconds. But this time, the pilot of the N0.5 helicopter came in a little too fast. His wheels skimmed through the water in the paddy, which is usually safe. But this time here was a dike under water that he didn't see. It tore off one wheel, and pushed the shaft up into the fuselage, ripping open the fuel tank. The helicopter didn't land, but stayed just off the ground while the troops got out. Then it headed back for Can Tho at full speed, gasoline pouring out of its wound. It would have been fatal to land there. This was the helicopter Perry was in.

The rest of us followed, above him. The flight was about 30 minutes, and there was great fear the helicopter's fuel would be gone too soon. But he made it. It was impossible to land, of course, because if a helicopter lands with a wheel gone, it spins around, tears itself to pieces and explodes. They tried first to build a cradle for it out of sand bags, but time was running out. Then the pilot tried to lad it on a sand pile. That didn't work either. I was right over it and expected it to burst into flame any second. But at the last minute, the pilot found a very deep, wide ditch filled with water. He lowered his machine very gradually into the ditch, being very careful not to let the rotor blades hit the ground. It worked, and the helicopter didn't roll over and blow up, and just came to rest. Fantastic good luck, and great piloting skill. Perry (and the pilot) are very lucky men tonight. Of course, the helicopter is a total loss, but that doesn't matter."

It was the most beautiful and frightening piece that I had ever read. It read like a war novel written by Hemingway with all the technical as well as emotional details. I worried for his life every time and yet his letters enlivened me and lifted my spirit out of my comparatively boring environment.

I had now lived and worked in Melbourne for two months. It was monotonous, and boring. We were as isolated as ever and most of the work was recopying articles written by Australian reporters into Vietnamese. I felt my brain was dulled and that I lacked any initiative or imagination. Apart from my friend Thai and the people from the Moral Rearmament, I had not met anyone new. My morale was low and I longed for news from Malcolm. It was not only a joy to let him seduce me with poetry, but also to refill my energy with his diversified philosophical and political comments.

For instance, after engaging in a dispute with his colleague (whom I prefer to keep nameless but to call him "X") Malcolm vented his anger by way of writing to me. The dispute was about Cambodia, and the opinions of the

American embassy people in Phnom Penh. According to X, these Americans did not want to upset the applecart by criticizing the Cambodian political regime because they – the Americans - had a plushy life there.

"...He (X) can't accept the idea that anyone ever does anything for the sole reason that they believe in it for its own sake.

I don't believe in very much myself. But I do believe in human beings. Whatever else they are, they are creatures who have struggled to raise themselves out of the mud, to create something more that the food with which they stuff their bellies. They are not content to live within nature as it was handed to them. They fight against the natural order of things, because they believe things can be made better. Yes, the cynic can tell me, 'but what have they done? They have made hydrogen bombs, rockets, and other gadgets with which they tear their fellow creatures to pieces.' Do you think I don't know that? I have seen enough of man's cruelty to man, to be disgusted with his human animal for the rest of my life. But I have seen the other side of human beings, too. The noble part, that reaches for the stars – and looks foolish and stupid when it slips on a banana peel and falls on its buttocks. It's very easy to make fun of belief in this kind of thing. The so-called 'idealist,' the man or woman who believes in anything at all, can be made to look like the most ridiculous creature that ever crawls the face of the earth.

And with this kind of thing in mind, if you give me a choice, for example, between President Diem and X, I would choose Diem instantly. In his way, Diem has botched up an awful lot of things. He has brought about cruelties and suffering in his people he will probably never realize. But Diem does believe in some things (perhaps the wrong things) and Diem tries. X believes in nothing, tries for nothing, if it seems too difficult. He is like far too many people springing up all over the world, people who have not the slightest reason for being alive, except that they happen to have been born, and resent the fact. They'd be happy enough to resign from life (with a pistol or razor blade) if it weren't so physically painful and troublesome. And somehow, there is a breed of foreign correspondent bums that falls exactly into this class. They are correspondents because they can use the position to attain a rootless, painless, comfortable kind of existence, in which anything goes.

Why am I boring you with all this? Because it matters very much to me, and you are the only human being really close to me, and you are the only one to whom I can write or speak exactly what I feel...

As for correspondents – I believe they hold a tremendous responsibility to be selfless, hard-working truth seekers. (Tell Trump how true it always is.)

Their lives are more interesting than those of most other people, but this is ncidental. There are too many of them who might just as well be shoe sales-nen. Weak, selfish people who want on physically agreeable adventure without ccepting the responsibility that goes with it.

If all this sounds like Moral Rearmament, it isn't. The point is, you nust be a realist, as well as a believer, and these organized nuts are not realists. The world does not become a better place just because you believe in sweetness nd light. You must fight for what you believe, with fire and steel if necessary.

And you will lose, because those against you are always stronger in this ind of fight – there are more of them. But even in losing, you pick up the word where you fell, and go on fighting. He will die too, but this the way the vorld goes. The first human being who suggested it might be useful to climb lown from the trees and try walking on two feet probably was hacked to death r his brothers, who thought living in the trees was better.

My darling, you tell me to be careful,…I know exactly what I am do-ng, and I know exactly what can happen to me if I slip on that banana peel. I m not the 'quiet American,' who tries to remake this world according to his wn image, with no idea at all about the things that really are going on around im. I am not proud, either."

That was my first lesson in a philosophy of life that I found a bit hard o take. I was one of these millions of people who were born to enjoy an easy nd comfortable life if I could. I had no ideology requiring me to sacrifice ny life for the country. My father was killed by the communists or by some ndividuals who took advantage of war to get revenge for themselves. I was herefore anti-communist and against any authoritarian regime that used pow-r to commit cruelties against its people, especially against innocent and poor eople. Malcolm's view of life reminded me of my father, gentle, generous, when necessary and very loyal to his country. And my father was killed for that.

Am I going to suffer my mother's fate? I mused and I worried. Being onest and realistic would not lead to happiness but defeat, even in love. There s no such thing as pure love. It would fade away as we grow accustomed to ach other, get bored, and begin fights and quarrels.

During my adult life, while single, I had to be aggressive and fight not nly for survival, but also for dignity and respect. I talked of fate and luck, but n reality, it was only a small part of the whole.

Malcolm seemed to take life too seriously. For that, he was different rom his colleagues and, I guess, he did not have a lot of friends. When I was till in Viet Nam, many times we were asked to join a group for dinner or

lunch, most of the time he turned them down. It was not because he wante
to be with me alone. If so, I should be flattered, and, who knows, I might no
have gone to Australia. I knew that he did not like to socialize a lot. If it wer
for some benefit to his job, he could break any appointment with me withou
any hesitation.

And being superstitious all my life, I felt I was constantly overshad-
owed by death and destruction, not my own but my loved ones'. I believe tha
more for selfish reasons than for piety. We live to suffer. Was it the Buddhis
teaching that I was taught by my mother? In one letter Malcolm analyzed m
in that way:

There are going to be times when I shall have to protect you fror
yourself – the hardest thing of all. If left to yourself, you would tear yourself t
pieces. You are like a powerful engine with no governor. If left alone, you star
running at top speed, aimlessly, exploding from your own inner momentum
No, I don't want to reform you, or change you in any way. I just want to kee
you safe from your enemies. And your worst enemy is you."

I was not sure whether he was right or whether it was a cliché that al
men used to seduce their girlfriends. After all, I was now independent with a
good job and a bright future. My mother and my sister kept pushing me t
look into immigration. They wrote me letters asking about life and custom
in Australia. They went to Malcolm enquiring about the Australian embassy.
They had counted on me to sponsor them to immigrate to Australia once I
settled down permanently. If my prospect was to find security and permanency
I could have it right there. I and my family could live there all our life without
worrying about war or poverty. And I might marry my friend Thai and have
my own family.

On the other hand, Malcolm might know me better than I knew myself. After two months of work, I began to feel depressed and unsatisfied. Melbourne was a sleepy town and nothing exciting happened there except for occasional sand storms. Looking back on my life in Saigon, I had the opportunity
to promote myself and to take the initiative on my own to further my career.
I met interesting and fascinating foreigners, including foreign correspondents.
Despite the rigidity of the regime, I had begun to become good friends with
my superiors and co-workers. I was able to help my family have a better living.
I had no doubt that I could get a job with any foreign companies or embassies
easily, being fluent in French and English.

In Australia, I was just a simple desk clerk. The job was dull and un-
inspiring. We broadcast the news and yet we didn't write or cover any event.

ll we did was translate what had been covered, and then read it. I began to egret missing all the adventures, including coups, political upheavals and war, n Viet Nam. I missed the adrenaline rush when some explosion happened omewhere or when the foreign correspondents poured in to my office for nformation or to get accredited. Also I missed going out to parties and official alas when foreign dignitaries visited our country, and I missed meeting new eople. And of course, I missed Malcolm.

His love for me and mine for him drew us closer and reaffirmed our rust to each other. If I didn't strike while the iron was still hot, I might throw way a true love that I finally felt deeply inside.

One day, I had a mild disagreement with my co-workers on some subect that I no longer remember. It prompted me to go and see the director. I sked to be relieved of my job.

"Why? Is there something wrong?" my boss looked surprised and puzled.

"No, I just want to go home and get married," I lied.

"You've just been here for two months," he complained, and I could eel that he was annoyed. I worried that he might remind me that I had a threeear contract with Radio Australia. "I can't force you. In principle, you have o notify us three months in advance." I figured out that by then I could save nough money for my air fare.

I was surprised when he agreed to let me go. He must have believed ne about getting married because gossip among the foreign press must have eached Radio Australia about Malcolm's and my relationship. That was the nly reason that he would have possibly let me go without making a fuss about ny resignation.

I suddenly felt relieved and my mood began to improve. I sent a cable o Malcolm and immediately received his cable: "open arms await you love."

CHAPTER SIX

Learning that I had given three-month notice to the "Voice of Australia," Malcolm immediately cabled me: "eye walking on air stop fate on our side forever now."

A few days later, a letter followed addressing me as "my Le Lieu, my little wife." Included in the letter I found a hand-made calendar with three columns starting November 1st to February 10th, the day I was supposed to leave Australia. That was in mid-October, barely two months onto my job.

In his letter, Malcolm mentioned that my sister had come to see him the day before. She had not learned yet of my intention to quit the job. She was eager for Malcolm to take her to the Australian Embassy to enquire about an entry visa. Malcolm showed her my letter and explained to her my decision to come back to Viet Nam.

The news came out of the blue. I had never been clear about my sister's intention to move to Australia. In my mind, I had thought that during her bad moods, she had looked for an escape. Now I had betrayed my family who had counted on me to bring them to Australia. Their dream was upended by my selfishness. But they had never expressed their wishes to me clearly, except for some hints that I took for pleasantries.

Even if I had stayed in Australia, I could not have financially supported the huge family, which, I figured, included my mother and the two brothers. And yet, I felt guilty and blamed myself for being selfish and insensitive. On the other hand, I was really unhappy with the job and the environment. My heart was not in my work and I became restless and impatient. I had never really liked my co-workers although, in all fairness, they treated me as member of the "family."

All said, I had never heard of immigration law. I was not even aware of such a thing as being an immigrant. Radio Australia had taken care of all the paperwork needed to get us here. We were only responsible getting a passport and a Vietnamese exit visa. In fact, I later learned that Australian immigration laws were even stricter than the American laws. An applicant could wait for years before being granted an entry visa. Ignorance sometimes shapes one's fate.

In the '60s, Viet Nam was more or less stable and safe despite some skirmishes in the countryside and grenade explosions in the cities. The Diem regime was more or less backed by the Kennedy Administration. My mother had her own teaching job. She had never expressed any desire to go to Australia to be with me. I could go on re-assuring myself that I had done nothing wrong by quitting my job. In reality, looking back at all the uncertainties during that period, and at what was to come in the future, I had to admit that it was a good move on my part.

As Malcolm said, fate was on our side. It was too late for me to change my mind.

I continued to work normally and patiently, knowing that it was just for a few more weeks. I continued to go out with Thai during week-ends; our friendship remained intact. I also decided that there was no reason for me to look for another place to live. On the other hand, Minh started to talk about looking for a boarding place for women to move out of the house. "It's not proper for me to live alone with the men," she confided to me.

Minh came from the North where she had a strict upbringing. She and I had not become close to each other in more than two months living together. I never trusted the Northerners. Like every Southerner, I was constantly reminded that Northerners would stab you on the back at any time that you stood on their way. Although we are one country, speaking the same language, sharing the same culture, and patriotic, we mistrusted one another. It had something to do with geography and environment.

In general, the North was so arid that rice farming was restricted to one crop a year. No other industries were properly developed. To survive meant to work, fight, deceive and cheat. The Southerners nicknamed people from the North "ca ro cay," wooden bass, making fun of them as people too poor to afford real fish to eat. Yet, out in Saigon society, they were driving Mercedes cars and owning sumptuous villas.

In 1954, after the French were defeated at Dien Bien Phu, the country had been divided in two. The communist regime under President Ho Chi Minh was installed in the North. Ngo Dinh Diem, backed by the French, ruled the South. Refugees from the North came pouring down south following their leader, the Ngo family. The majority were Catholics. Preferential treatment was bestowed on them as they were resettled in the South with land, jobs, and housing. Most members of Diem's cabinet were made up of his followers or those who were willing to convert to Catholicism. That caused animosity between Northerners and Southerners. I had friends whom I had known since childhood, trained as engineers in France, who were forced to convert to

Catholicism in order to gain managerial positions as engineers.

Diem and his brothers only trusted their followers. There was constant resentment by the Southerners of injustice and usurpation of power. They believed that the Northerners were land-grabbers and fortune-seekers. We, from the rich South, were accused of being lazy and spoiled. We didn't need to work to live. All we did was lie in bed all day and then by meal-time, just stretch out our hands to pluck up 'the fruits of nature" growing around us. We were characterized as frank, honest, generous and naïve. There was some logical explanation of the differences between the two sides. One came from the arid land where starvation sprang up every three years or even more often.

I even remembered, one special year during my childhood, overhearing my parents and their friends discussing a famine in Hanoi. It was so bad that dead bodies were strewn in the streets. I saw pictures in the newspaper of sanitation workers pushing wooden carts loaded with bodies. We lived to eat, while the Northerners worked to live.

I digress here, all to explain my relationship with my co-workers who were all from the North.

Minh had a mild disposition, reserved and cautious. It turned out that we had a common friend, François Nivolon, the correspondent for "Le Figaro" who would later be Malcolm's best man at our wedding. François was also Minh's best friend. I even maliciously suspected, although without any evidence, that they might be more than friends. It was woman's intuition, and I accused myself of being as bad as any other female gossipers. I thought Minh was not interested in any romantic commitment.

Being over 30, Minh was tall and slim. Almost a year my senior, she was quite good looking and friendly. She did not wear any cosmetics, and looked older than her age. She always looked so serious, and her humor was dry and sometimes sinister.

"I never trust men. They are smooth talking but incapable of taking responsibility," she told me one day. I learned that she had lost her parents at young age and had to work to support her two brothers. It was only recently that the brothers had become independent, and she was freed to pursue her career. She was working for a French bank when she heard that Radio Australia was recruiting Vietnamese for the project.

Minh loved to talk about love and marriage as if they were things missing from her life. She boasted that she had been proposed marriage many times but had turned it down because of family obligations. She was sarcastic and coarse whenever the subject of men came up. She laughed at my weakness in sacrificing my career for love.

"Another love letter from Malcolm?" She sarcastically remarked whenever the mail came in. "Men! Don't they leave us alone? I wouldn't sacrifice my career for any man."

"It's because you haven't met anyone you really like so far," I sniffed.

"They tell you that they love you, but they often lie to take advantage of you," Minh ruminated sadly. Whenever the subject of love or men came up, Minh could argue for hours. In turn, I suspected that she must have been lonely and had been deceived on several occasions to be so obsessed with the subject.

One evening as we prepared for bed, Hung came to ask my permission to go through my room to see Minh. They must have had some kind of argument during supper, and I presumed he wanted to apologize. I noticed that he sat on a chair next to her bed and they talked for a long time. At the end, Hung smiled coming out to tell me that everything was all right.

A few months after I was back in Viet Nam, a couple of strangers came to see me with baskets of fruit and cookies delicately wrapped in red cellophane with decorated red ribbons, a Vietnamese tradition of bringing gifts to friends, as a way of announcing an up-coming matrimonial celebration. I was so stunned to learn that Minh and Hung were engaged and soon after got married. They must have been in love while I still lived with them and might have decided to get married sooner so to solve the housing problem.

What was the anti-marriage and anti-men talk that Minh had fed me during our confidential talks? That was an example of the kind of phony pretense I mentioned before.

Hung, the supervisor and Minh's secret love, was also from the North. He had lived in England for ten years and worked for the BBC. He confessed that he was very unhappy in Viet Nam. He was 36 years old and tried to hide his baldness with awkwardness and embarrassment. He combed his hair in such a way as to cover more or less the nakedness of his forehead. Some early mornings, I caught him wearing a hat as he walked towards the kitchen for coffee. I averted my eyes as if I didn't see him: however I was amused by his display of vanity.

I liked Hung, perhaps because he had lived abroad and behaved more like a gentleman. He was not more than five feet two or three inches tall, and his skin was transparently white. His manners were gentle and businesslike. He was agreeable and simple to be with. He took pains in everything he did and never complained. He liked to cook and took charge of cooking dinners for thers. Once I stopped eating with them, I never had any problem with Hung. could see that Minh and Hung were a good match.

Nostalgically, I assumed that my co-workers must have dispersed to ifferent places by this time, and the house must have been vacated. It was just n idle thought without any related regret. I might be the culprit or the cupid who had precipitated the marriage of Hung and Minh, so consumed by my wn upcoming departure that I had no time for diversions. I was making plans o travel home by ship to visit other ports along the South Sea. By then, I had tarted saving to pay my passage back.

Letters from Malcolm came almost every day and kept me entertained. n November, he wrote that he had two weeks of vacation coming up and he ery much wanted to come to Melbourne to take me home. At the time, his oreign correspondent's salary was adequate to live comfortably, though not o travel much, and he also had a wife and child in America to support. Nev-rtheless, he believed that he could save enough by the time I was to leave in ebruary.

I was not very enthusiastic about having him come to Melbourne be-ause I did not feel comfortable enough to openly admit to my Vietnamese olleagues to having an affair with him. They knew that we were engaged but had never offered any further information beyond that. I still wanted to take leisure trip home by ship to take the advantage of visiting different places in outh Sea. The cruise might take more than two weeks to get to Saigon. For Malcolm, that would exceed his allowed vacation days.

By mid-November, I received a letter from Malcolm saying that he was orced to take his previously arranged two-week vacation because his office had lready found a reporter to stand in for him at that time. He planned to spend t in Hong Kong where he could stay with friends and save on expenses.

The idea of spending two weeks in Hong Kong excited my imagination. had never been anywhere in Asia except Viet Nam and Cambodia. I had often eard through my encounters with foreign correspondents that Hong Kong vas a heavenly place. They always described it as the most exotic and romantic lace to live. I also saw the movies "Suzy Wong" and "Love Is a Many-Splen-lored Thing." The scenes in these two movies were enough to make me dream, vith an American journalist (played by the handsome actor William Holden) n love with a Chinese woman (played by the famous Jennifer Jones.)

They were my two favorite actors. In "Love is a Many-Splendored Thing," they met in Hong Kong and fell in love. She played a medical doc-or who came from a family in communist China living in Hong Kong, the heroine had her family in communist China. (The movie was made in the 60s when Hong Kong was still a British colony.) She was torn between love of an American and traditional family. Love, of course, conquered and then tragedy struck. The American was called to cover a battle and was killed while typing his news report under a tree.

I started to compare my situation with that in the movie. Malcolm was a war correspondent covering the most dangerous guerilla warfare in Viet Nam. Until now, my love life was considered a failure. I lived in fear of losing Malcolm because of the war. Impulsively, I wanted to be with him in Hong Kong.

So the idea of spending a few days there with Malcolm before going back to Viet Nam started haunting my sleep. I knew that once back in Viet Nam, I would have difficulty getting an exit visa to go anywhere. As long as I was outside with a passport, this was a chance for me to travel. But I was not due to leave until February as set when I had submitted my resignation.

I became obsessed with trying to find an excuse to leave earlier. I had already broken my contract with the "Voice" and was lucky that my resignation had been accepted. Every day, I visualized myself walking with Malcolm along Hong Kong's streets, eating in good Chinese restaurants, shopping among the jewelry rows that were so often compared with the treasures of Ali Baba.

Once more I was struck with luck. The third of our Vietnamese staff who had delayed his coming for over a month suddenly showed up. We had almost forgotten about him. Duc was a jovial man, educated in the USA, and enjoyed drinking in bars every evening, during his one-hour break. I jumped at the realization that an added member who could replace me was here.

My intimidation and shame gave way to an uncontrollable impulse. Time was running out. Malcolm was going to start his vacation the day I finally whipped up courage to confront my superior.

"Is there anything wrong Le Lieu?" the manager looked up when he saw me enter his office.

"May I see you a minute," I said, my face burning with shame.

"Yes," he said, putting down his pen with a bit of annoyance.

"Now that Duc is here, I feel bad to ask, but I'd like to leave earlier."

He stared at me, firmly pressed his lips and looked ready to chase me out of the office. I was myself ready to run away, fearing that he might insult me or retract my resignation. He sat for a moment, piercing me with his blue eyes and calmly smirked.

"I see. What's the reason now?" I breathed with relief and utterly hameless I told him that I wanted to join Malcolm in Hong Kong.

"I see. So we are back to Malcolm now?" I kept my eyes on the floor.

"Hong Kong is certainly a beautiful place to go for honeymoon." His one of voice softened as he spoke, as if he had remembered something from he past.

"He is there right now," I said, feeling encouraged. "I know that I am upposed to leave some time at the end of January. But Duc is here and the vork is slow."

"Duc's position is radio-man and not administrator." He became annoyed. I kept silent.

"So when do you want to leave?"I looked at him in surprise and at the ame time noted his desire to end the interview.

"Malcolm's vacation is only for two weeks. I would much appreciate it f I am allowed to leave within one week. It gives me time to put things in order nd to arrange for the travel," I said sheepishly. He silently looked at me with a tone face. My heart was thumping with embarrassment and dread.

"Just show Duc your job, although, again, he is a radio man. I'll try to ind some replacement soon."

"I am sorry for the inconvenience," I said, about to apologize and express my appreciation for his kindness when he cut me short.

"Do you have a date?"

"November 25th?"

"Good luck and congratulations," he told me, stretching out his hand o shake mine.

I walked out, relieved and excited. Back in the office, I happily announced my sudden departure to my co-workers. They surrounded me with ongratulations and wished me a happy future. I spent the rest of my day looking up the airline schedules. I called Quantas to get more information. There vas no direct flight to Hong Kong from Melbourne. I had to change planes in ydney. I booked the flight for November 25th. There was a connection from idney to Hong Kong the same day.

When I told Thai my departure date, he looked grim but silent. I was orry for him because he had counted on me to keep him company. Although ve had been dating for over two months, I did not know much about him nd his life. I was being careful not to be too personal or to touch on any ubtle subject such as love or romance, fearing to offend him. On the other hand, he never ventured to reveal his personal history or his real feelings toward me. I had always regarded him as a good friend. My departure meant he would have to find another companion.

As the date of departure approached, I received a letter from Malcolm in which he enclosed a letter from Ann, his wife. In summary, she asked him to delay the divorce process because she was looking for a job, and it would look better on her résumé if she were married to Malcolm. I was disappointed, but empathized with her difficult situation.

"I am doomed," I reflected quietly, accepting whatever fate had for me. Malcolm's love was enough to nourish my dreams.

So November 25th came with anticipation. The forecast for that day was stormy in Melbourne. My connection to Hong Kong was scheduled two hours after landing in Sydney. "Plenty of time to change planes," I muttered. Thai drove me to the airport in the storm. I breathed with relief when the flight was on time. Thai and I hugged each other in silence. Thai kept his stoical mask, straight and unsmiling while a battle of emotions, excitement and guilt was tearing my insides.

Thai was my "raison d'être" for over two months in that hole. I owed him a lot for keeping my sanity and for being kind and understanding. He was the platonic male friend that I had always wished to have. And here, once more, I said good-bye to a dear friend as the plane roared up the runway. This time, I didn't have time to sit and reflect on my life. The plane was right in the eye of the storm. It bounced up and down, left and right while the rain tried to rush into the window, threatening to engulf us all. The plane was half-empty and I had the luck of sitting beside an unoccupied seat. I lifted the handle between the two seats and was able to lie down and shut my eyes, feeling sick and praying for the storm to stop.

I survived the trip but missed my connection in Sydney, and there was no other Qantas flight to Hong Kong for two days. But there were other airlines flying there that night, if I were willing to risk being put on the waiting list. It would be around 9 in the evening Sydney time. I was tired and burdened with luggage. Lingering at the airport all day did not appeal to me, and the airline staff stated that flights to Hong Kong were always fully booked up far in advance. I was also upset by the disrespect and inconsiderateness they showed toward me as an Asian woman traveling alone.

I expected sympathy and commiseration for missing my connection. Instead, they looked upon me as a strayed immigrant and offered no help unless asked. I was told that, even if I wanted to go to Hong Kong two days from then, I was still be put on the waiting list because the plane was already booked up. I didn't want to risk of getting stuck in Sydney more than two days. I was miserable and so sick after such a turbulent flight that I decided not to stay in Sydney, but to fly directly to Viet Nam that day.

Once more, doomsday. Misery had turned into desperation. There was no flight to Viet Nam out of Sydney for two days, and then I would have to make a connection in Bangkok. There was no direct flight to Viet Nam for a week. Within five hours, my life was turned upside down. I felt like a poor, defenseless deer in the Australian jungle, threatened to be devoured by ferocious wild wolves.

Defeated and disgusted, I gave up and demanded to be put in a hotel room for two days while I waited for the flight to Bangkok. They put me in the YWCA at the center of town. I sent a cable to Malcolm and spent the rest of the time shopping and touring the town.

"Cheer up, Le Lieu! Wouldn't it be an opportunity to visit the famous City of Sydney before leaving for good?" Unlike my usual doom and gloom, I decided to be positive. I used my two days to explore the town. Two months prior, I and the rest of our Vietnamese team had spent our time here in meeting and sleeping. I hardly saw Sydney and its usual famous tourist sights. So at least now, I could boast knowing Sydney if asked. It was like any big city in Europe with high-rise residential and commercial buildings, tree-lined trees and well-decorated and expensive department stores.

It was in those department stores that I spent most of my time, buying household goods to bring home. When the day came to go back to the airport, an Australian air-steward came to pick me up as agreed in advance. He saw me burdened with packages and offered to help. He deposed me at the ticket counter and walked over to the clerk. I overheard him telling the clerk to charge me extra luggage. "Thanks a lot for your help," I sneeringly yelled out as he walked away smiling.

Nina Arnett met me at the Bangkok airport. I had two days in Bangkok before I could get a flight back to Viet Nam. Nina generously invited me to stay with her. It was more than half a century ago, and it's hard for me to remember details. I must have been in an exhausted state of mind. Nina was a Vietnamese who had dated Peter Arnett, a New Zealander and Associated Press reporter under Malcolm in Saigon. We knew each other through our boyfriends. Nina was married, at that time, to a Thai whom she had met while she was student in the US. Nina and I shared a lot of adventures once we were back in Viet Nam. Being a devout Buddhist, she and her family had participated in antigovernment demonstrations along with the monks. Eventually, she divorced her Thai husband and married Peter, who was awarded the Pullitzer

Prize in 1967 for his AP war coverage.

Finally, finally, I landed at that memorable Tan Son Nhat airport. I didn't expect Malcolm to be there. He was not due back from vacation for two more days. But my mother and the family were there to greet me. Le Lai introduced me to her third newly-born boy, who looked up at me with his big round eyes. Alain was the image of his father, big black eyes, abundant black hair, and a beautiful dimple when he smiled. I immediately took him in my arms in the taxi that took us to my old cottage. Through the alley, the landlady stuck out her head through a side window:

"Welcome back, Miss Le Lieu! Is he your baby?" her voice boomed out to be heard by our neighbors. She then cackled.

"No, he is my sister's boy," I answered in a rush to get into the house. Suddenly, I was red fuming at such a venomous and obnoxious greeting from that woman.

"What's the matter?" my sister looked worried.

"That vicious woman asked me whether Alain was my boy," I shouted back at her,

"Calm yourself. She is just an ignorant gossipmonger," my mother smiled sweetly as she looked for a place to sit down.

"Yes, I am home, sweet home," I murmured to myself as I was climbing the steps to my bedroom. The family prepared a sumptuous meal to welcome me back. My family was eager to know about Australia and the work I did. They also informed me that they had tried very hard to get "the Voice of Australia," but failed because they did not have a shortwave radio. Nobody seemed to be interested in knowing about my relationship with Malcolm. (Or if they were, I might have forgotten the conversation.)

"You have come back in time to attend Thuong's upcoming marriage," my mother said softly. Her eyes blandly stared at my brother with a forced smile on her lips.

The news took me by surprise and speechless. I couldn't believe my ears that brother number seven was engaged to the girl who lived on our block in Ben Tre. Before I left for Australia, he had vaguely mentioned her beauty and expressed his interest in her. I thought, at that time, that it was just a piece of idle conversation as we lounged around together at home. It turned out that it was much more than a tease.

Lan was the daughter of a jeweler who was one of our family's enemies, though he lived on our block. He had turned communist during the brief period of national independence in 1945. My mother considered him partly esponsible for the arrest of my father. I was also told that he had been the one /ho had told us to move to Cai Quao if we wanted to see our father again; the ommunists would place him under house arrest if he lived with us.

When the French retook Ben Tre, Lac-Thanh, Lan's father, took to the nderground along with his two teenage sons. They secretly came back after he Geneva agreement divided the country in two in 1954. He was sick and vanted to die among his family in Ben Tre. Before he died, he placed a bottle f camphor on the table and wrenched out of his sons a pledge to go back and o fight with the underground. His children ranged from 19 to 5 years old at hat time. We had gone to the same kindergarten and elementary schools and rown up together. But we always regarded them as our enemies and avoided heir company.

But somehow, my brother Thuong and Lan managed to keep their ecret love from all of us. Even my mother, living two houses away, was dumb-ounded. I was told that, during my absence, Thuong had confessed to her his ntention to marry Lan. My mother was strongly opposed. Being a good son the only good son among all the boys), Thuong did not press on. Lan wrote to ny mother, saying that she loved him. She had nothing to do with her father nd her two brothers and their politics. She would accept my mother's objec-ion with sadness. She had decided to sever her relationship with her family by lemanding her inheritance. Her elder sister chased her out of the house. Lan ook refuge in the convent in Dalat, hoping to become a novice. A good friend f my sister who happened to be a nun there then contacted her.

At first, my mother was still firmly opposed to the marriage. "I have lways told all of you that that family was our mortal enemy. They destroyed ur happiness and killed your father," she said, with tears in her eyes. Thuong ppealed to my sister to have a word with my mother: Lan had carried out her romise, and she had been in the convent for two months. Taking pity of the irl's youth and her son's emotional distress, my mother finally agreed to go vith Thuong to Dalat to bring her back.

For marriage, as in any Asian family, Lan needed to have her family's pproval. We had learned later that her eldest sister, Hai, who had inherited the ewelry store after the death of their parents, had also opposed the marriage. Hai used her siblings as paid employees with a small monthly salary, especially an, whose part of the inheritance was conditioned on her running the store. he went back to Ben Tre to inform her sister of the up-coming marriage and eclaim her share. Her sister called her a traitor, and Lan took her to court to laim her heritage.

“How come nobody wrote me about this when I was in Australia,” asked, feeling left out and a bit put off by such a tragedy.

“We didn’t want to worry you,” my sister replied while Thuong stayed silent.

‘All ends well. You are here,” my mother said, cutting short further discussion.

The marriage took place without any member of Lan’s family. Somehow, I was not surprised. Such a drama was seen in almost all Vietnamese households. Civil war had caused disruption and adversity. Hardly a single family in Viet Nam escaped that kind of “Romeo and Juliette” drama and family dysfunction. The majority of families, North and South, had family members working for the “wrong” side of the country, whether that side was communist or anti-communist.

Many Vietnamese young men and women of my generation were seduced by the Viet Cong propaganda and promises of a brighter future in an independent country. I was dragged into that when I was in school. Left-wing students were constantly demonstrating openly and disrupting our schooling. I was lectured by my brothers’ friends about the corrupt regime under the French-controlled territory. I should stand up for injustice, and blah…blah… blah. I could have been bent to their persuasion if only my father had not been killed by them.

So I was fully aware of the dilemma for these young people, especially those who lived in rural areas. On both sides, they were under ideological control. Now history is repeating itself. That’s what is happening in the Middle East as we speak. My father naively believed the same doctrine and did not get a chance to prove his nationalistic loyalty. (As an aside, when I was in Viet Nam in 2016 and spent a few days in “Cu Lao” island, known during the French colonial period as an asylum for leprosy victims and for political prisoners, I visited some “museums” which were actually nothing but old empty dilapidated prisons. I happened to be staying in a villa whose owner rented bicycles to tourists. I complimented her on her beautiful house, on a lovely tree-lined road. She said that the government had awarded to her for fighting against the Americans.)

During the ‘60s, with the American military buildup, the war had rapidly intensified. Thousands of young men on both sides were killed, leaving widows to raise their young children alone. In rural areas, people lived in fear of being kidnapped or arrested in the middle of the night, if not by the Viet Cong, then by government troops. Human life was cheap. Many children grew p in divided families, without fathers and without proper educations. I was ıst part of that. This is a wound I have that will not ever heal. When I see ref-gees pouring out of Syria or Iraq with children drowned or starved, my heart oes out to them. Malcolm's motto was "War is a Way."

I was happy for Thuong but shared my mother's emotions. In the end, ny brother had to drop out of college to support his family of four children. Ie was killed in 1972 while commuting from Saigon to a small town to teach. Ie left children ranging from three months to eight years old. Lan and the hildren moved to live with my mother until 1975. After the fall of South 'iet Nam, Lan, who like many strong Vietnamese women was a shrewd and xperienced businesswoman, paid smugglers for a passage on a boat to Hong .ong. The boat took on water far out at sea and they could have all drowned, ut fortunately, a Swedish ship came to their rescue.

Her sister, who was married to an American, sponsored the family for nmigration to the US. Her children grew up to become professionals -- an ngineer and a dentist -- and entrepreneurs. That was back in the 1980s when ıany Vietnamese refugees, the "boat people," were risking their lives to escape 'iet Nam. That was another epic that had affected and taught me a lot about uman resilience in the face of catastrophe and suffering.

On the other hand, my brother's entanglement in a family feud had wakened a sense of belonging in me. The moment I got back from Australia, I ıstantly knew that I had done the right thing. I was a different person.

Thinking back on the two years I spent in Viet Nam before going to ustralia, I see myself then as a young rotten child, thrown into a jungle of olitics and intrigue without any vision or direction. I was self-centered, with npredictable impulses. I had forgotten the reason why I had come back home rom Europe in the first place. I was so alienated from the way of life In Viet Jam that I blocked out any criticism coming from my mother or family. I ecame obnoxious and arrogant. My small salary was enough to provide a roof or me and my two brothers and daily meals, but I was almost never there to ave any serious communication with any of my family members.

Then I flew away, defying family love and responsibilities. I didn't give thought to what could happen to my mother and the family. Thinking only bout myself had consumed all my energy. Now, ironically, love had trans-ormed my personality and molded my character. Love had strengthened my onviction that there were good and positive things in life.

I didn't realize that my absence of three months in Australia had de-rived my family of a regular income. I didn't save enough to send money back to them. Besides, I was too unsettled and insecure in my work to think of my family's welfare.

Now, back with my family, I realized that I had neglected my first duty to take care of them. I promised to be a better person. I resumed my responsibilities as the eldest daughter and sister. I had Malcolm's assurance that he would hire me to work for him. For the first time in my life, I gained self-confidence and self-reliance. I felt needed and I looked forward to a new life.

Malcolm returned two days after me. I need not describe how heavenly our reunion was. I stayed with him overnight in the little apartment above the AP office.

Before we parted the next morning, Malcolm gave me an envelope on which he had typed: "A long letter to Le Lieu written lonely Wednesday night after she missed the plane. Things I wanted to say to her but couldn't at the moment."

I read the words on the envelope with foreboding. It was a five-page typewritten letter.

"Sorry about the letter," he told me. "I want you to be aware of things that might counter our hope. And that's the reason I wrote the letter while I could think clearly."

"So it's good-bye?" I waved the letter in front of my nose.

"Yes, good-bye until tonight, silly girl," he took me into his arms and kissed me passionately. "I love you and I forbid you to use that word ever."

The letter was like a contract of marriage with reassuring words of love and trust. Malcolm spelled out four points that might affect our future life.

> *1. Malcolm anticipated my disappointment at missing the flight, and the gloom and doom that I so often felt. "What worries me sick is that now you have some feeling that everything must always go wrong. Oh baby, if only I were with you and could convince you things will be all right."(I was amazed by how well he could read my mind.)*
>
> *2. There was that dark thought hanging on every correspondent living in Viet Nam – that he/she might be expelled within twenty four hour notice. That could separate us again, although he reassured me that he felt confident that his reporting was fair and honest. "In my year in Viet Nam, I have not learned the language but I have learned a great deal about VN politics. I am not a completely naïve, blundering 'quiet American.' Anyone reading*

all the stories I have written in Viet Nam would see immediately that I have never been politically involved on any side."

3. AP might assign him to another country before the divorce came through. He maintained that he had been prepared to wait for three years when I was in Australia. There was no reason for me to fear. "The moment I was free I would be back to marry you (just as if you had stuck in Melbourne for three years – I would have been down there within 12 hours after my divorce became final)."

4. My mother might object to the marriage because, he wrote, I quote, "I am a frivolous young man with two broken marriages who will bring nothing but grief?"

The letter concluded with words that I could have expressed myself although not so eloquently and movingly as his. "I claim you now, as my woman, and give you myself as your man, and yours alone. We are our own family now, neither the family of my parents or your parents. The Hudson and the Mekong are going to blend (easily, because identical water flows through both of them) whether anyone likes it or not. You are a brave, wonderful person to come back to me, despite the difficulties and inconveniences and criticism from others. And you have done the right thing, don't forget it. You came back because you have faith in me, in our love and in the future. We have already won our toughest battle. Life is beginning for us now, my little wife."

It was the happiest period in my life. Despite war, atrocities, political upheavals and death, I was at peace with myself. I was fulfilling my duty toward my family and was closer to my mother. I caught up with her, learning more about various childhood stories I didn't know. She filled me in on my father's life, of which I only remembered pieces here and there.

Life with Malcolm in Viet Nam was a learning process of adjustment and adaptation that stimulated and enlightened my intellect. I could have lived a quiet and boring life in Melbourne. Instead, I had experienced the most exciting life as soon as I stepped back into the Viet Nam arena.

"When you marry a correspondent, you become, like him, a citizen of the world. It is never goodbye to any place, but only au revoir." Malcolm wrote these words to win me over, although perhaps he did not know that the Viet Nam war had shaped his career and propelled him to celebrity.

And I lived a life that I had never even dreamt could be real.

CHAPTER SEVEN

I was ready to take life into my own hands. I no longer had any doubt bout my limitations or my own destiny. I was back on my own turf. I was reed of contracts and obligations. Well, that is not completely right. Malcolm ad mentioned having me work for him. He reiterated his promise by fixing a ate for me to start.

Following his instructions, I showed up at the Associated Press office he next morning. The office was on the ground floor in the same building where Malcolm's upstairs lodging was located. As I entered the office, Malolm was in lively conversation with David Halberstam, the New York Times orrespondent. He spotted me and indicated an empty chair near the door. Halberstam turned around and boomed: "So, here is Miss Le Lieu, the new AP reporter!" Heads turned in my direction. I felt my face turning red with mbarrassment. How did he know about my working for Malcolm? I thought t was personal business.

In general, I mostly got along with foreigners, journalists, diplomats, eachers and entrepreneurs. And yet, I was uncomfortable with Halberstam nd I sensed that he echoed the same sentiment toward me. And here I was, nfortunate enough to run into him on my first day at work.

So I twisted my lips into a smile and defiantly waved at other friends tanding behind him. The office was packed with visitors and they all seemed o be talking at the same time.

The windowless office was about 16 feet wide and 25 feet long, with a mall bathroom at the back. It was pleasantly cooled by a constantly droning ir-conditioner mounted above the door. Its claustrophobic atmosphere of cigrette smoke and its stale smell intensified my intolerance level. Apart from he narrow entrance passage, the whole space was taken up by two small desks rranged at an angle, in addition to a table with an enormous typewriter/fax nachine against one wall, and another small table, for the clerk, facing the wall eparating the bathroom. I sat at the end of Malcolm's desk, close to the entrance. Malcolm gave me a piece written in "cablelese," with words abbreviated or combined to keep down the cost of sending. The flow of visitors, mostly ournalists, made such a commotion that I kept wondering how could anyone oncentrate on their work.

The racket they made fascinated me and, at the same time, rattled m
nerves. After an hour sitting there, looking more and more bewildered an
out-of-place, I discreetly removed myself to take refuge in Malcolm's apart
ment upstairs. Malcolm wouldn't have time to train me. If he wasn't on th
telephone, he was busy typing out articles, take 1..., take 2... (more cabl
jargon, meaning second page or third page on a working article, each "take
being sent separately.) Journalists, visitors, out-of-towners stopped daily by t
read the news or to chat.

"It's a heavy day," Malcolm said when he came up to check on me afte
a while. "There was rumor of some disturbance in Hue, some protests by th
Buddhists. You see, darling, with a wire service, I have to be on guard 24 hours
so as not to be beaten by UPI. And these nuisance reporters, like Halberstam
come to read my copy. I don't have time for them but I am obliged." He sa
down next to me on the couch and lit a cigarette. I always disliked cigarett
smoke and the smell. But at that period, almost everybody smoked, includin
my brothers. So it was a norm that was part of social life.

"Why do you let them do that? Aren't they supposed to do their ow
reporting?" At that time, I was still ignorant of the differences between wir
services and newspapers.

"They pay wire services to share their news reports. I don't always le
them read everything. You will learn more and more about wire services as yo
go along."

"I don't believe so, darling," I said. He didn't say anything. "I kno
that you are trying to help me and I appreciate your generosity. I am in you
way, and, besides I don't know anything much I can help you with. I feel a bi
out of place and ridiculous."

"You'll learn. You are an intelligent girl," Malcolm's voice was not con-
vincing.

"You can't afford me any way," I hugged him tenderly. "I am not worried about jobs, truly. All I do is to wave my magic wand and presto, jobs fal
into my lap," I said with confidence. "If you need me to translate something
you can always leave it in the apartment. I'll help, but I don't want to be i
your hair."

"Don Hewitt, my boss, will be here in one week," Malcolm said. "I ca
ask him permission to hire you. You are much more observant and intuitiv
than Tran. Despite his perfect English, he could not separate important new
and trivial things. I am sure AP could afford you," Malcolm insisted.

Don Hewitt came a week later. As an exploratory introduction, w

ent out to dinner with him. I disliked him at first glance. It had nothing to
o with his job or social behavior. He struck me as a derogatory type who had
ved for a long time in Asia and assumed a superior attitude toward native
aff. About 60, stiff, with grey hair and a grey moustache, he spoke with a
ight southern accent. I did not pretend to know enough about America to
idge at that time. Despite my past experience with various American journal-
ts, I still had a hard time identifying different regional accents. On the other
and, I had heard a lot about racism and prejudice in the South. That might
ave triggered my instant dislike of Don Hewitt, perhaps just pre-conception
n my part.

Having met him just for dinner, I had no impression of him beyond
he image of an old grey-haired man. He had come to check on the AP staffing
nd used the opportunity to do some public relations with the Vietnamese
overnment and with AP overseas subscribers. I predicted in advance that he
ould turn down Malcolm's request to hire me. And I was right.

"Don't worry, baby," Malcolm tried to console me. He put his arm
round my shoulder as we sat on the couch. He took out a pack of cigarettes
rom his shirt pocket and shuffled out a cigarette with the other hand and put
in his mouth. He picked up the lighter on the table and lit it. Malcolm was a
eavy smoker at that time and it had always provoked my aversion and distaste
oe the smell.

"I have been asked to do some extra radio reporting for AP. You may
e of use to me from time to time. Besides, I am due for home leave in April.
hope to be able to bring you to New York to meet my parents. So don't think
f any job right now."

The idea of going to New York immediately perked me up. I had saved
ome a small amount of money in Australia. With the rate of black market
xchange, I still could afford to provide financial support for my family for at
east a few more months without worrying about jobs.

True to his word, I was given a tape-recorder and a microphone. One
ay Malcolm asked me to go out and record all the typical noises of Saigon.
Vith that heavy recorder on my shoulder and the microphone on hand, I
valked the streets. I recorded the tap-tap of the wooden sticks that the noo-
lle-cart vendor used to announce his presence. I went to some night-clubs
o record Vietnamese songs being sung by popular Vietnamese singers. My
ecordings also included the deafening noises of motorbikes, cars honk-
ng, the hullaballoo of the central market, church bells, pagoda gongs, the
hanting at the Buddhist temples and children's screams of joy and cries of

pains in small parks around the city.

Despite the heat, the heavy recorder and the long walks, I felt inspirec and useful. Once I had accomplished my mission, Malcolm worked on th narration. So whenever he was too busy with fresh news, he assigned me to re cord any activities related to radio requests. Once he played back the broadcas that was diffused in New York for me to appreciate the teamwork.

The Buddhist protests in Hue started to attract foreign press coverage They had started when the Diem regime forbade public gatherings to celebrat Buddha's birthday in central Hue on February 8, 1963. That provoked protest and anti-government demonstrations. Within one month, the crowd had ex panded to include students and members of other institutions. Malcolm decid ed to make a trip to Hue to assess the situation. Every day, we learned of riot and police arrests. The pagodas in Saigon started stirring with small gathering within their compounds. I, a Buddhist myself, felt outraged and applauded th courage of the people of Hue. Hue's governor was an ardent Catholic, an iron glad ruler. He was Ngo Dinh Can, one of Diem's brothers. He was the mos hated and brutal fanatic among the brothers.

Hue was earlier the royal city where royal palaces and temples wer erected in the 19th Century. Bao-Dai, the last in the royal blood line, wa crowned and designated Emperor of Viet Nam by the colonial French gov ernment. The majority of the Vietnamese people were Buddhist and prou of their origin. If we disliked Northerners, we, from the South, respected an regarded Hue as the birthplace of Viet Nam. It was from there that we defeate the Han invasion over two-thousand years ago.

So cancelling such an important celebration was, in the eyes of all Bud dhists, an affront to the freedom of religion. The whole country in the Sout rose up. In Saigon, the monks began to organize. Nina Arnett and I separatel attended some of their meetings. We also brought back news from the pagoda to our newsmen. Malcolm predicted that it was going to be a long civil war be tween Buddhists and Catholics. Most Vietnamese, including me, were hopin that the American government would intervene to overturn Diem's incursior into the freedom of religion.

Rumors of impending coups and anti-government plots exploded ever day among the Vietnamese communities. They were angry when the American kept silent, and wondered why. We were living in an unstable and dangerou time. The South Vietnamese Buddhists condemned Diem and his family fo blasphemy and disrespect toward our traditional religion. They were determine to defend the monks by defying curfews and denouncing police brutality.

During the whole month of February, Buddhist demonstrations got bolder and bolder, even blocking the main arteries of Saigon. Chanting monks, followed by the faithful, slowly sneaked out of their pagodas, avoiding Secret Service spies, to gather at a designated place in the city, but notifying foreign correspondents the day before. Malcolm believed that it was safer for me to stay with him than to go home at night. He predicted that it was going to be all out civil war. I was thankful I was no longer part of the government. The AP office turned into a gathering place at night for the staff to review the events of the day and to dissect the situation with vivid arguments and debates.

One day, Malcolm came home to tell me that the monks had asked all the foreign correspondents to come at around five in the morning because "something very important" was going to happen.

The journalists showed up on time, but came back two hours later disappointed and sleepy. They were told to come back the same time the next day. And still they were left empty handed. The same promise was made the next day and the next day, for five consecutive days. On the sixth day, almost all the foreign journalists gave up, tired of being used by the monks. The journalists accused the monks of abusing their trust to advance their political ambition and to influence their cause to the world. But Malcolm persisted in attending the morning meeting, partly because of his deep commitment, as a reporter, to see through the fight and partly because of my profound faith and conviction that the country was united to defend the cause to the end.

"What do you think it will be?" I anxiously asked Malcolm as he was getting dressed at four that morning. "So far, it has been peaceful - Buddhist policy. Is there going to be a coup? Would some courageous military general be there to declare war against Diem? Are they going to massacre the monks?" So many nightmarish ideas had haunted my daily preoccupations.

"I don't think it will be a coup. But who knows? I sense something more sinister, but I can't put my hands on it. On the other hand, it may be nothing, just as it has been these last days. Go back to bed, don't worry," Malcolm said as he was ready to leave, his old box camera on his neck and his bulky tape recorder slung on his shoulder."I love you. Go back to bed. See you later." He kissed me and closed the door behind him. I went back to bed, praying and worrying.

By eight o'clock, I waited for Malcolm to come back for breakfast. I turned on the radio. There was nothing about a demonstration. By noon, he came back, sweat running down his sad red face.

"A monk just burned himself," he told me, and hugged me tight. "I

can't look at food. The smell of the burning flesh is still fresh in my nose. I hav
to go down to send pictures. You can come down if you wish."

I followed him down to the office. There were other journalists ther
and the office was in a big commotion. I spotted Nina Arnett among the news
men. She was crying and I hugged her, tears coming down my cheeks. I neve
felt so close to Nina as I was at the time. We shared our faith and our pains.

"You two should go in hiding," Malcolm turned around to tell us afte
he came out of the dark room. He showed us several pictures of the burnin
monk. Tears continued to pour out as Nina and I looked at these horribl
images.

"I have to find out some way to send these pictures quickly. I worr
about you both. It's not safe here for you. Nina, you should not go back to you
family tonight."

"She'll come with me. I feel that the police don't know where I live.
Nina thanked me and accepted. I left her lingering at the AP office while I wen
home to let my family know and to arrange accommodations for Nina.

The whole story was recounted in Malcolm's book Muddy Boots &
Red Socks. His photograph earned him a World Press Photo Award, and wa
nominated for the Pulitzer Prize, but lost to the photos of Lee Harvey Oswald'
being shot after Kennedy's assassination. With the prize, Malcolm bought a
engagement ring from Amsterdam and proposed, on his knees. I was so move
and humbled by his love.

The burning monk picture made history in America. It was said tha
President Kennedy saw it at his breakfast table the next day. Mme Nhu, th
fiery First Lady, fueled the flames by calling the dead man a "barbecued monk
during her last visit to the USA. She not only shocked the Vietnamese, bu
defied President Kennedy. Apparently it was her rhetoric that caused Kenned
to signal his support for a military coup against Diem.

Malcolm, who went to the airport to cover Mme Nhu's departure t
the United States that day, came back to tell me that he was very moved by th
sight of her husband, Ngo Dinh Nhu. According to Malcolm, Nhu just hun
back alone, gazing at the airplane. "I bet that he was saying farewell to her, a
if he were not going to see her again."

Malcolm's instinct was correct. Mme Nhu never saw her husban
again. He and his brother, President Diem, were killed a few days later in
bloody coup.

Malcolm never ceased to fascinate me with his profound knowledg
of Viet Nam's politics, and his love for the country. In 1975 we were living i

elgrade, the capital of Yugoslavia at that time, when the Vietnamese city of Kontum fell to the Viet Cong. When Malcolm heard the news, he turned to me and confidently declared that Viet Nam would be lost forever.

"How can you tell?" I was a bit startled at first and I light-heartedly added: "Kontum is just a village. It has no important strategic importance, except for the Montagnards. Remember the 1968 Tet Offensive, when Hue and Saigon were under attack by the Viet Cong? We survived, didn't we?"

"Yeah, that was a mistake on their part. They have learned their lessons. They should never attack big cities. This time they took the whole village. That's the beginning, mark my words." After that, Malcolm went to his office and sent a cable to the New York Times expressing his concerns. The day after, the Times requested that he go to Viet Nam immediately.

He was right all along. Two weeks later, I received a cable from him saying I should come to Saigon to rescue my family. I went to my sister who lived in France and asked her if she could take in our mother in her home. She was skeptical, and I was still not fully convinced that Viet Nam was lost. I took an Air France flight the next day for Saigon. As we were approaching an intermediate stop in Beirut, I heard my name on the loudspeaker. I was to get off there. I almost had a heart attack; my eyes filled with tears as I had horrifying visions of Malcolm and my whole family being taken prisoners by the Viet Cong.

The New York Times Beirut bureau chief told me over the airplane phone that he was just following Malcolm's orders. He had reserved a room in the Commodore Hotel for me. When I got there, though, it turned out that they had nothing available and they sent me to another hotel nearby. I called the Times bureau chief, whom I never actually saw in person (I don't remember his name), and he said Malcolm had told him he was worried that Saigon could fall before I arrived. The Times man thought that it would be best to get me off the plane until Malcolm called with more news.

Saigon had not fallen, in fact. I sent Malcolm a cable, being upset myself for being pulled off the airplane, and booked a seat on another flight the next day. Malcolm was upset when he found out what had happened. Perhaps his colleague had misunderstood him. Lebanon was in a civil war and Beirut was every bit as dangerous as Saigon. Going around on foot, I saw many military checkpoints similar to the ones in Saigon. I could have been kidnapped or trapped in fighting in Beirut, never mind Saigon.

When I finally got there, I immediately went to see my mother. All my brothers and their wives were there, anxious to know whether I could get them out of the country. My family consisted of 15 members including some dozen children ranging from four months to seven years of age.

I didn't know anything about welfare or refugee status in the United States, as I had never lived there myself. Malcolm kept telling me that with that family size we might have a financial problem. We lived outside of the United States and therefore had no way to accommodate them. I had no money of my own and could not possibly let Malcolm take on the charges.

Meanwhile, the Viet Cong and the North Vietnamese Army were surrounding the capital. Refugees kept pouring in by every means of transportation. As the New York Times photographer, I was allowed to accompany Malcolm wherever that was safe. With a small charter airplane, we chased news all over places that were still free from the invaders. I and Malcolm covered the flow of refugees arriving by boats in the beach resort of Vung Tao. We stepped into a boat where a dead mother had wrapped her dead baby in her arms, and other bodies were scattered all over the upper deck. The boat stank with the pungent smell of decaying flesh.

I felt as if I had disrespectfully invaded a sanctified place. At another place, a group of starving people fought over a loaf of bread. I saw a four-year-old child waddling alone with piece of bread, so I plunged into the crowd to snatch a package to hand it to the child. Malcolm angrily dragged me away fearing that I could get lost among the crowd.

Coming back from Australia, I had expected to lead a peaceful life Instead, I lived in the most historic and dangerous time in South Viet Nam Coup after coup persisted after the death of Diem and his brother Nhu. Rivalries among the military forces and the huge American military buildup created endless conflict. For that and for the rest of the Viet Nam war, I refer to Malcolm's book for deeper reporting on the period of 1960s, and the experiences Malcolm and I shared until the dénouement of our marriage life.

As the Vietnamese military took power in Saigon with the coup against Diem, calmness settled in for awhile, except for occasional rivalries among generals.

Malcolm took me to New York on his home leave. My first reaction while we were driven from the airport to Manhattan was dismal. We went by one huge cemetery after another, and Manhattan itself looked like the biggest of all of them, enlarged by 200 times, with its skyscrapers, steeples and monuments thrusting upward. The sidewalks were made of concrete, denuded of trees or flowering plants. No city parks or shady public roundabouts were in view at first sight. (I was so used to beautiful Paris and London, where there

/ere public parks within a few blocks wherever you went. Besides, it was in 963, before Lady Bird initiated the idea of beautifying the cities.)

AP took advantage of Malcolm's sudden celebrity to promote its work, nd his. Malcolm had to give lectures in different towns, leaving me with his ıother, nicknamed Manya, at 70 West 11th Street, in Greenwich Village. I 'as struck by her emaciated body and by her wrinkled face, which made her ›ok like an old woman though she was only fifty-five years old. She walked ke a ninety-year-old and struggled for air because of her emphysema. She eemed to live on cigarettes and coffee.

But she put me at ease right away. Besides, being a stranger and not nowing the culture of the country, I felt a bit embarrassed and self-conscious bout being Malcolm's girlfriend, as he was still married. Manya welcomed me /ith open arms. Once I got back to Viet Nam, she wrote me loving letters, ddressing me as Le Lieu Browne. She openly accepted me as her daughter-in-ıw.

Malcolm and his mother shared many common interests in life. She vas an accomplished pianist. She used to play at a small, but famous theater n the Village. She was an intellectual who yearned to travel and see the world. ife was not kind to her. Being brought up along with her sister by a single nother who was an art teacher, Manya had a hard life. Her mother set up a pri-ate art school at her house in upstate New York and took in boarders. Manya ooked for twenty students and maintained the household.

She met and married Malcolm's father, one of her mother's students. he dreamt of traveling and meeting interesting people. Instead, the family fell o poverty during the Depression. With four children to raise, the family was onstantly being displaced from one location to the next. Her husband finally ound employment at Pan American World Airways. Being an architect, he vas absent from home so often that the responsibility for raising their children ell to Manya.

When I met her, she looked frail and lonely. I noticed that she en-ertained a lot: most of them were friends or colleagues of Malcolm but total trangers to her. I felt that she missed human contact, especially the intellectual ind. She read a lot and was very well informed about daily events within the ountry as well as overseas. I was sorry not to have known her for long or to be ble to be a comfort to her during her last part of her life. She inspired me to herish every moment I was with my own mother.

Back in Saigon after New York, Malcolm plunged again into the Viet-ıamese political turmoil. The power struggles between military generals kept the country on edge. In addition, the Kennedy and Johnson administration started increasing the number of American troops to fight the Viet Cong. It be gan from some 10,000 American advisors and grew to 75,000 troops by 1964 and 125,000 by early 1965. Constant military operations and bombings daily had left the country ever at war.

Malcolm spent a lot of time either with the Vietnamese military in operations in the Delta, or with the American special forces. Each day, he lef the apartment by dawn and did not come back until after four or five in th afternoon. Each time, I spent my time praying or expecting the worst.

One day, he told me that he was going out with an American helicop ter group. American helicopters were known to be constant Viet Cong targets They were shot down so often that the news of a 'copter crash was routinely considered serious only when the body count was high. That day, I turned on the radio expecting news. Instead, "Symphonie Fantastique" by Berlioz was on It was the last movement, where "Dies Irae" starts slowly punctuating note by note to announce the approach of death.

"Could it be an omen?" My blood froze. I felt chills running down my spine. I was obsessed by possible mishaps and disasters, convinced that I was destined to lead a miserable life. That day, Malcolm came home shaken. He was with American forces when their helicopter was shot down, an event vivid ly described in his book Muddy Boots and Red Socks. That kind of nightmare wait-and-pray, was constantly with me until 1966 when we departed from Vie Nam, we thought for good.

After the brief home leave with Malcolm, I decided that it was time for me to get a job. My mother was to retire soon. My youngest brother had been drafted and was in military service in Nha Trang, in coastal central Viet Nam He was scared and threatened to go AWOL. My sister, who happened to know a high-ranking officer in Saigon, managed to get him pulled back to Saigon where he was reassigned to work in the Presidential Palace.

I applied for jobs with the famous French Shell company and with the US Information Service, USIS. I picked USIS because it not only paid better, but also the office was situated two blocks from home. It was again one of the best jobs I ever had. I was assigned with the Publication section where propaganda leaflets and magazines were published. My first boss was a typi cal bureaucrat whose passion was hunting. Fortunately his term ended a few months later, and he was replaced by Frank Eaken, a mild mannered and mod est person. He was short and loved his tobacco pipe. He was kind and friendly to the staff. He made me his assistant, responsible for having all Vietnamese ublications translated into English. He gave me a free hand to hire outside ranslators. Most of all, he assigned me as a local reporter for USIS monthly nagazines.

Along with a staff photographer, Khanh, we travelled all over the countryside in an office car, visiting local factories, farmers and local craft industries. It was the first time that I had learned the process of lacquered-furniture naking. I spoke with local farmers and entrepreneurs. Once a week, Khanh, who came from the South and was knowledgeable of the safety and security of he Southern part of Saigon, would guide me where to go and with whom to peak.

We interviewed lacquer artists and learned how to process "nuoc mam" fish sauce,) as typical of Vietnamese cuisine as soy sauce is to Chinese. Sometimes we had to cross by sampan to the other side of the Saigon River during a ow tide. To get on dry land, we were forced to crawl our way out in mud, and requently slipped and fell while trying to climb up a muddy coconut trunk to each the top of the bank. We were drenched with mud, but had a marvelous ime.

Once back in the office, I wrote stories in my bad Vietnamese vernacular. The best was that I had a senior editor, a professional journalist, who took ny stories and turned them into readable and poetic pieces. He never criticized ny writing during the whole time I worked there. I had no complaints. The nagazine was popular among farmers and rural people. Once again, destiny ad worked in a mysterious way.

I also had a unique opportunity to accompany a group of outstanding Vietnamese students chosen by USIS to visit the famous aircraft carrier Intrepid," which is now a museum docked in New York. The Intrepid was ending planes off to bomb North Viet Nam at that time. It was an extraordinary expedition for me (jealously envied by Malcolm, who had never obtained he permission to visit it as a journalist). I was scared but thrilled by abrupt ull of the helicopter landing on the aircraft. I and the students were treated s VIPs. We were escorted and given explanations of the ship's operations. We nterviewed pilots, watched the airplanes being catapulted off and then landing nd being brought to a stop by arresting cables. I felt privileged and yet also listurbed by the thought of hundreds of innocents being victims of the powrful bombs they dropped.

By 1964, Malcolm shared a Pulitzer Prize with David Halberstam, and ook me along with him to New York to receive it, although I had never heard f the prize before. AP took the opportunity to set up several lectures to promote him in various states. Earning a good reputation, Malcolm was offered job with ABC, and a book contract.

It had been known among the foreign community in Saigon and amon my co-workers that Malcolm and I had been living together. I was self-con scious of my awkward situation. I felt I had disgraced my family, particularl my mother, in regard to her friends. I confided to her, and she suggested tha I should think of common-law marriage as a solution. Common marriage wa regarded in Viet Nam as legal, and legitimate. It was up to the families of th bride and the groom to approve the union. Relatives and family friends wer invited to an often elaborate party. The newly-wed couple would be introduce and would receive blessings and gifts from guests.

After consulting with Malcolm, who had no objection on it, invita tions went out to announce our wedding. In Saigon, the whole foreign pres and friends of Malcolm and my family attended our party. My mother als organized a wedding party in Ben Tre for her friends and neighbors. I did no let Malcolm attend the ceremony in Ben Tre, as a precaution. We did not wan to attract attention in a hostile environment. Friends and acquaintances starte calling me Mrs. Browne.

Between 1963 and August 1966, Malcolm won a Pulitzer Prize a World Press Photo Prize, the Overseas Press Club Prize, the George Pol Award, a Sigma Delta Chi award and other smaller prizes. He was shot dow three times, had his feet injured by stepping on bamboo spikes, and endure multiple smaller mishaps. He left the AP in 1965 to work briefly for ABC, an published the **Face of War**. And, after leaving ABC, he contributed monthl articles for the now-defunct men's magazine **True**.

In June of 1966, Malcolm was accepted for a fellowship of the Counci on Foreign Relations in New York. In the same month, out of nowhere, w received news that his second wife had decided to give him the divorce. So w were officially wed in July at the Saigon City Hall. A month later, we packe and sent our dog, Nif Naf, a Japanese spaniel my brother gave me, to New Yor prior to our arrival.

Nif Naf was barely one year old. He travelled all over the world wit us as long as we lived overseas, then and later. He was gassed in the streets o Viet Nam, bombed in Cambodia and during the India/Pakistan war. He wa submitted to a body-search at a London airport and at other airports all ove Eastern Europe while it was still behind the Iron Curtain. He was so trauma tized by bombings and shootings that, late in life, he screamed in his slee at night. He loved airline food, lived in four-star hotels and ate room-servic ıeals. And he was spoiled rotten by international hotel managers' wives.

When Nif Naf died in New York, Malcolm and I drove to Vermont to ury him in our old country house in Ascutney. We could not help but cry all ıe way, in particular at places where we remembered stopping to let him out ɔr a walk. We never owned another dog.

New York, in 1966-1967, was more dangerous than Viet Nam during ıe war. We lived on Gay Street in a tiny apartment in the Village. Roaches cudded everywhere and dropped down on my face during my sleep. We were urglarized, threatened by homeless bums, and pickpocketed at Macy's. I had ever been scared or felt unsafe in Viet Nam. In New York, on the advice of ıe police, Malcolm bought me a shot-gun to defend myself at home when he as at work at The New York Times.

I was on the verge of using it one morning. Coming out of the shower, till naked, I heard a noise and saw the door knob turning. I yelled out that had a rifle in my hands. I heard the foot noise receding down the staircase.

In Washington, I was harassed by a redneck near the White House on ennsylvania Avenue. When Malcolm was invited to lecture at some universi-ies in the South, we stayed in the host's home so to avoid hotels and unpleas-nt encounters with racists. We witnessed race riots in Los Angeles, and Viet Jam war protests almost everywhere.

As the Fellowship at the Council on Foreign Relations ended after a ear, Malcolm was hired by **The New York Times** as a foreign correspondent. Ie was assigned as Bureau Chief in South America, starting in January, 1968. Ve both could not wait to leave that hole in New York. Even by the time we rrived in Buenos Aires, half of our hand luggage was missing. Malcolm was ight when he told me that he hated New York and would never want to live here. I was delighted when I heard it.

I was prepared to be a foreign correspondent's wife, a life that I had hought to be beyond my reach.

Vietnamese team with Radio Australia members in charge of Voice of Australia.

Sister, Le Lai Richard, with her toddlers, France and Dominique, and me.

Malcolm receives the World Press Photo Award at Amsterdam in 1963.

Joined JUSPAO (the renamed U.S Information Office in Saigon) in 1964.

U.S. Chargé d'Affaires William Trueheart receiving condolences from Vietnamese students after President John F. Kennedy's assassination.

Mrs. Malcolm W. Browne, with many kind regards
Henry Cabot Lodge

U.S. Ambassador in Saigon Henry Cabot Lodge pays a visit to JUSPAO staff.

Reporting trips outside of Saigon for the JUSPAO Magazine.

Malcolm (in the middle) with his grand-mother, Donna, at his right and his mother, Manya, at his left after Boris, his Russian friend.

Le Guillaume Tell

MENU

-:-:-:-:-:-

LE CONSOMME FROID EN GELEE AU PORTO

LA QUICHE LORRAINE

LE TOURNEDOS ROSSINI

LES POMMES NOUVELLES VAPEUR

LES HARICOTS VERTS AU BEURRE

LES COEURS DE LAITUE A L'HUILE

LA GLACE FINE CHAMPAGNE

LA TARTE AUX POMMES

LA DEMI TASSE

-o-o-o-o-o-o-

SAIGON, le 12 Août 1966

Farewell party for us from the Saigon Press Club.

CHAPTER EIGHT

In general, I took life as it offered itself. I was happy to have someone
take care of me, and all my worries disappeared. Malcolm's tolerance toward
y frivolity and my laissez-faire attitude might have contributed to his despair.
ow that I know the truth of his tortuous past, I accuse myself of being too
lfish. He must have felt lonely and resented my aloofness. And I sailed along
noothly, carefree and unconcerned. I thought that he was the commander
nd I was just following. I lived under his shadow and tried not to interfere
ith his career. No wonder there were so many alcoholics and divorces among
reign correspondents in that golden age of journalism. Journalism is an un-
ppreciated job. It's true that it is an interesting life. I can't deny that Malcolm
nd I had a unique life in the sense that we were unseparated despite some
ormy periods. But there were also many happy and exciting times we had
gether. Let me now return to the time when we returned to New York after
x years of covering the early years of the war in Viet Nam.

From 1968 to 1987, Malcolm's beats for the New York Times took us
South America, Pakistan and what was East Pakistan then and now Ban-
ladesh after its gaining independence; South East Asia, Eastern Europe, the
oviet Union and the Middle East. The places we covered included Argenti-
a, Chile, Peru, Paraguay, Bolivia, Uruguay, Brazil, Colombia, Easter Island,
awaii, Cambodia, Thailand, Laos, Yugoslavia, Rumania, Poland, Hungary,
zechoslovakia at that time, Bulgaria, Slovenia, Finland, Pakistan, Afghani-
an, Nepal and Iran.

Malcolm went alone to places where danger loomed too close for my
wn safety, such as Nicaragua, Saudi Arabia, the Tunisian Sahara, and Mexico.
alcolm's favorite place was Antarctica. He went there five times but could not
ke me along because civilians were not allowed in military bases there. For
acations, we hiked to the base of Mount Everest; we visited Egypt's pyramids
nd their surroundings; Morocco, New Zealand and China.

Half of our overseas life, we lived in hotel rooms with our pre-packed
ggage. Intercontinental Hotels were our favorite because they tolerated dogs.
e were lucky to be able to confide our Nif Naf to the hotel housekeeper
anagers while we were away. Due to the wars in Indochina, and in Pakistan,
e were constantly on the road too much to have a permanent place for our-

selves. The New York Times allowed us to make our home in hotels, with ou belongings. So for several years, we kept hotel rooms in Bangkok, Laos an Cambodia on a permanent basis. In Pakistan, former President Zulfikar A Bhutto, during the Pakistan/India war, retreated into a hotel room across fro ours. He even came over one night to talk with Malcolm. Bhutto was assassi nated a few years later.

Going from one hotel to the next, I had the illusion of being a ric tycoon, living in the most luxurious places around the world. Many of m female friends sympathized with my situation, assuming that I felt depriv with no permanent home. But I had appreciated such a life. Everything was a my disposition: spas, swimming pools, highly-rated restaurants, chambermaid and soft beds. I had never missed cooking or shopping. I even daydreamed o finishing my life in such a fashion, an apartment or a penthouse in a luxuriou hotel such as the Plaza in New York! Of course, it was just an idle fantasy o fairy tale, or else presumptuous wishful thinking. It's more likely I'll end up i a senior citizen institution; that is to say if I am lucky enough to afford eve that.

To help pay for my travel with Malcolm, I became his news photog rapher. He showed me the technique and how to work in a darkroom. In stantaneously, I was accepted and my pictures frequently appeared in the Ne York Times, complementing Malcolm's articles. Suddenly I became aware tha I had turned into a threat and a competitor to other freelance photographers In the '60s and '70s, female correspondents were very few. In South America if memory serves me well, there were only two, one a freelancer and the othe working for the Italian press. I was Malcolm's sidekick. We worked as a team although Malcolm was the boss.

We were bombed in Karachi during the Pakistan/India war. We wer harassed by the KGB in Moscow and by secret police in Hungary and Czecho slovakia. We were evicted in Chile. Besides facing dangers ourselves in riot and fighting, we saw death and misery around the world. In "Red Socks an Muddy Boots," Malcolm wrote enough for both of us about his experience in world politics, wars and harassment by foreign as well as American govern ments when they did not like his stories. Here, I'd like to share a few anecdote that affected me personally.

Among the countries that we covered in South America, Bolivia wa our favorite place. If we talk about the third-world, Bolivia had all the char acteristics: poor, politically unstable, autocratic rule and communist-incline government. But it was the most colorful and picturesque country. La Paz, th apital, is on a high plateau at an altitude of 13,000 feet, and its airport is at 4,000 feet. On first arriving there, when we disembarked from the plane, we oth struggled to stay on our feet, as we could hardly breathe for lack of oxy-en. Many of our correspondent friends told us that they, too, almost passed ut every time they got off a plane. I was awed by the sight of a soccer game hen the airport bus passed by a field. The players were running around, kick-ng and jumping as if they were at sea-level, while we were pumping our lungs or air.

La Paz was more a little town than a capital city. Its population was 0% Indians from the Inca tribe. The main street consisted of a fairly good otel and one or two restaurants, a few shops and a beauty parlor. Further p the hill, there was another cheaper and quieter hotel, with a daily mar-et nearby that I was drawn to. I liked to explore the exotic, native products hat were displayed right on the dirty ground. There were silver heirlooms, ncluding sets of teapots, silver pots and pans and trays. I assumed that these nerchants had been forced to sell their heirlooms to support their families. hese items must have been in the family for generations. The market was run y native Indians; the women wore mostly multiple-layer white or red long kirts, with mixed-colored lace shawls wrapped around their shoulders. The nen wore knee-high coarse-fabric pants and a kind of casual jacket, and often overed their heads with knitted bonnets. The temperature in the Andes was nild during daytime and cold at night.

On our first trip to La Paz, we were lucky to be invited to ride with President René Barrientos on his helicopter to his residence. I was the only woman, surrounded by the President at one end, and his staff and military dvisors on both sides. I remember Barrientos pleasantly addressing me in per-on, but nothing about what he said. A few months after our encounter, Barri-ntos was killed in a plane crash. He was the President who captured and killed he famous guerilla Che Guevara, and I liked him at first sight.

Once we got used to the thin air and were able to breathe normally, we vanted to explore the High Plateau, or Andi-Plata. We rented a car and drove ut of La Paz on a dirt road. For miles, we only saw vast empty desert, with few green patches of agriculture. It was an eerie, mystic atmosphere, like an nchanted mirage, with the dark, purple Andes surrounded by the vast sandy lain. At the border with Peru, we crossed through a small village with a few ry-mudwall houses. We stopped in a small restaurant for lunch, and for the rst time I saw those exotic llamas, a cross between a horse and a deer and used s beasts of burden. Their coats, long and wooly like fur, were used for blankets or carpets for sale as souvenirs.

In Peru we continued on our dirt road for some hundred miles to reach Lake Titicaca, the highest lake in the world. It was so immense that where the sky met the water, it looked domelike. The water was clear and calm. A few native peasants leading their cute llamas along the edge of the lake added to the colorful landscape. I felt that we were between heaven and earth, mysteri ous and serene. A wooden ferry was waiting for us and our car to board. Two men, one on each side of the ferry, steered it with long poles. (I keep won dering whether modern equipment has ever reached that region, as tourists with cheap airfares, might by now have invaded that remoteness.)We were exhausted and out of breath because of the thin air. But it was an adventure that I never forgot.

Later there was another opportunity or rather another circumstance that drew us back to the region.

While covering Peru, we had decided to visit the famous Machu-Pic chu on our free week-end. There we made friends with an American FBI tour ist, a man named Westfall from Texas, (I forget his first name,) and a young newlywed English couple. We planned to fly back to Lima the next day. Back in the hotel, we heard over the radio that the Bolivian military had taken over the government in a coup d'état. That was big news, and it was happening in Malcolm's beat. He immediately tried to book a flight to La Paz, but unfortu nately, as would happen in any coup, all the airports had closed down.

The only way we could reach La Paz was to drive some 800 miles in dirt road, plus crossing Lake Titicaca. It would take two days, if all went well.

Our new friends had heard Malcolm's plan and wanted to join in by sharing the rental car with us. We started at dawn. About 100 miles out of Lima, we encountered a check-point. At first, Malcolm and I feared that the coup in Bolivia might be the reason. It turned out that there had been some kind of epidemic and that the Peruvian sanitation department had set up the checkpoint to spray all travelers. Despite our protests, we had to spread our arms and legs to be submitted to antiseptic spray, right in the middle of the road. We felt humiliated and yet quaint.

After 12 hours of driving and crossing Lake Titicaca, we reached the border with Bolivia as darkness fell. Exhausted, we looked for hotel rooms only to be told that the only available possibility was to share a common room with others. We were shown into a large room occupied completely by an enormous wooden bench that served as a bed. I was horrified to see several local men deep in sleep in one corner. I instinctively walked out, determined

› sleep in the car. Malcolm and the young woman talked me into going back › the room. I was to sleep next to Malcolm at the end of the bed. The snor- ıg, the smell of sweat and bad breath in such an enclosure made me so sick ıat I hardly closed my eyes the whole night. At some point in the middle of ıe night, I heard a noise like someone cocking a rifle or some other kind of rearm. Malcolm confirmed my suspicion in the morning. He had also heard but did not want to alarm me.

By the morning, we had learned that La Paz airport had reopened. Malcolm and I were disheartened – we had missed the coup despite all our fforts. In addition, we were all suffering from the high altitude. Our fellow avelers were sick and had difficulty breathing. Despite our prior experiences ı such an environment, we, too, were in a poor state because of exhaustion. ut we had to push on to La Paz along with the sick and groaning passengers ı our car. It was a pitiful sight, but I could not help but feel proud of our re- lience and endurance.

When we reached the capital, Malcolm immediately got to work de- ›ite the altitude and fatigue to catch up with events. Fortunately, the hotel here we often stayed had rooms available for us and our friends. We were also verjoyed to learn that the competition was also late arriving. Malcolm filed his opy and it made the front page in the New York Times.

Our fellow passengers disappeared for the night. Sleep was the only ay to counter high-altitude sickness. If memory serves me right, the three of ıem left La Paz the next day after thanking us for the trip.

A month later, we received a crate of Campbell's canned soup sent ia a Merchant Marine ship coming from Texas. Westfall, the FBI man, was ıe sender. Malcolm, during the voyage, had confided to Westfall how much e missed Campbell's., which we could not find anywhere in that part of the orld. We were very grateful and touched. We continued corresponding with im for many years.

The reason I tell this story is that because a correspondent is responsible ›r covering a vast area, when a crisis occurs, the immediate response that is quired often involves hardship and stress, not to mention danger.

Most of the time, the people whom we encountered randomly turned ut to be the nicest ones, compared with diplomats or government elites or oliticians. I was so used to having Malcolm on my side that I forgot how vul- erable I might be without him. Two examples had taught me about life alone. somehow got engulfed in fights with (mostly) authorities on both sides of the cean, Viet Nam and the USA – my birthplace and my adopted country.

In the 1970s, the government of South Viet Nam required visas fo foreign correspondents, and often, when the visa expired, they had to leave th country, go to a Vietnamese consulate and get a new one. Not being a journalist, I could enter and stay one month, but if I intended to stay longer, I had t go through the bureaucratic process of bribing immigration officers to have m visa renewed in expedited time, from twenty four hours to two days maximum Without the bribe, I could spend hours at the immigration office, and it migh take days. I couldn't even be sure of getting an extended visa. To avoid all th headaches, it was better for me to fly out every month to the nearest country Hong Kong, Bangkok, or Singapore, and to return after a week abroad. I opte for Hong Kong as my anchor for obvious reasons.

As arranged in advance, once I decided to come back to Viet Nam afte a few days away, I called the New York Times office in Hong Kong to ask then to let Malcolm know the date so that he could pick me up at the airport. O one occasion, for some reason, the NYT secretary mixed up the date of m return. I arrived at Saigon airport and did not see Malcolm there. I though that it was simpler to hail a taxi instead of phoning him and waiting for hin at the terminal. I went through a thorough luggage search and inconsequentia interrogations. I expected such a humiliation because the Vietnamese custom officers were famous for their corruption and bad behavior towards Vietnamese women holding American passports. It was a national prejudice and racis attitude that I have already mentioned.

As soon as the taxi left the airport gate, two policemen stopped th car. The driver jumped out and automatically opened the trunk as if it was routine search. One policeman opened my luggage and slowly lifted each item took it in his hands and examined it closely on different corners.

"I just came out of customs, there is no reason for you to search m luggage again," I got out of the car and watched him going through my luggage, item by item.

He did not respond but started to pick up a can of China tea. He slowly examined it, turned it sideways, upside down, then opened it and smelled it

"Boy! The way you search my luggage, I suppose that you also do suc a good job when you encounter a Viet Cong." I was in such a rage.

"What do you say about the Viet Cong? Are you pro Viet Cong? O are you Viet Cong yourself? You better come to the station with us." And h ordered me into the car and ordered the driver to follow his car. Before getting into the car, I caught sight of an American serviceman coming out of th American base across from the airport. I yelled to him to telephone my husnd, Malcolm at the New York Times office. Instead, he shook his head and lked away.

"You should have given them 200 piasters (worth $10 US dollars) and ey would have let you go," the driver complained as he drove us to the station lf-a-mile north. I suddenly remembered that all taxi drivers had to work with ese corrupted police along this route. I was enraged by the rottenness of my vn people and defied them to arrest me.

They took me into an empty room at the police headquarters and left e there. I was within my rights; and holding an American passport, I was no mood to play their game. The room was completely empty of any furture except for two chairs. It was bright and aerated with several windows. ne walls were whitewashed and completely devoid of pictures. I just calmly t on a chair and waited. An hour passed. I didn't even bother to try to open e door or call out to anyone. I just wondered calmly how long they would eep me locked up. Malcolm was, of course, in the dark. I figured out that the ong Kong bureau must have forgotten to send the cable, or it had mixed up e dates. Malcolm would have been at the airport to meet me. He knew the ietnamese police too well to leave me stranded.

At last, someone came in and asked me to follow him. He was in cilian clothes and very polite. As soon as I was invited to sit down at his desk, e took out a form and shyly whispered to me the same thing the driver had ld me. But he demonstrated some sympathy and just asked my name and ldress. He didn't even tell me what I was charged with. Pressed by me, he mply answered that it was a misunderstanding. I would be discharged as soon s the minister signed the release. I remained at his desk. A few minutes later, saw a car pulling in and I was politely asked to step out to meet the minister. Ie was in the driver's seat, and signed the form handed to him by the clerk. Ie shook my hand and apologized for the misunderstanding. He drove away nd I was guided to the taxi driver who had patiently been waiting for me in ne parking lot.

It was all a scheme to make money, and the driver had been their acomplice. I asked him to take me to the New York Times office. Still fuming vith anger, I entered the office while the driver carried my luggage in. Malcolm ooked up from his typewriter in surprise.

"Hello there!" he got up and came towards me. "I thought that you vere supposed to return on the third." He kissed me and guided me to a chair. In any case, I am happy that you are here now."

"I was detained by the police for two hours," rapid enraged

words poured out of my mouth.

"What was the matter?" Malcolm asked anxiously, as Sydney Scha berg, another NYT correspondent, approached me. "You were arrested? Why

I told the story. Malcolm and Sydney listened quietly. As soon as finished, Malcolm turned red with fury, rubbing his nose with his two hand a sign of uncontrollable anger. He quietly went over his desk, took a piece blank paper and fed it into his typewriter.

"Tell me again slowly. I am going to send the story to the New Yo Times immediately." He looked as if he was going to hit somebody.

"Wait a minute," Sydney intervened. "I should write the story, not yo for obvious reasons. You are Le Lieu's husband. Calm down. I've heard enoug to send out 200 words on the incident right away." He walked over his des "Why don't you take Le Lieu back to the hotel. She needs a rest after such traumatizing experience. Trust me. The story will be at the Foreign Desk with in 30 minutes."

True to Sydney's words, a story about my incident was published in th New York Times the next day, with harsh words about the police corruptio The foreign press had heard about this kind of corruption before, but the never had any evidence to write about it until I became the victim. It was bittersweet revenge for me although my conscience was deeply troubled.

Having worked for the government, I was fully aware that these po licemen were poorly paid. They might have a large family to feed and I wa considered as being in a privileged class, travelling abroad and marrying a so called rich American. Life in Saigon during that period could be risky, too But unchecked, this kind of corruption played into the hands of profitee and fraudsters. To survive, one had to build up one's own safety net. It was Charles Dickens world, luck and instinct played a big role in shaping one's fate Cheating and lying might not be virtues but that was the way of life. Bein honest could land you in jail.

All my life, I was somehow mostly shielded from miseries and ugli ness of the world – luck or destiny. Miraculously, I was spared disastrous acci dents that might cause physical harm and mental tortures. I was always honest speaking from my heart, and yet naïve in my outlook. I trusted anyone who was friendly or kind to me. Once I had Malcolm on my side, I let go all my reserve and suspicion. In his profession, he was the one to watch out for al the traps and ambushes that might be set against us. Left to my own devices, made mistakes and got myself into a jam.

For instance, one evening in early 1973 we were dining with some merican diplomats in Phnom-Penh. I was sitting next to a young charming merican who seemed to appreciate the food and the ambiance of the place. learned that he worked in the immigration office of the Embassy. I had been lanning to visit my mother, but worried about the North Vietnamese stamp aat was in my American passport.

A month earlier, after the US and North Viet Nam had reached a cease-re agreement and pressured South Viet Nam's government to accept it even 1ough it allowed the communists to keep the parts of the country they had oc-upied, the news came that soon all American prisoners of war would be freed 1 Hanoi. The foreign press was invited for the occasion. Our group, about ome twenty American correspondents and television personalities, chartered a aotian plane and flew to Hanoi. For me, it was a most exciting and emotional rip to be present in enemy territory as a news photographer for the New York 'imes. At the Hanoi airport, going through the passport check, I felt faint. I eared that I might be either expelled or detained once they found out that I vas Vietnamese. The officer just took all our passports and led us to the bus. hey would return our passports when we left at the end of the day. It was one day expedition under the communists' guidance. They took us to the Ianoi Hilton (nickname for the prison where American prisoners of war had een detained.) There, row after row of American prisoners dressed in uniform toically stood at attention while we took their pictures. We were not allowed speak to them.

We were permitted to accompany them by bus to the airport, where 1ey would board a U.S. C-130 plane home. It was a very moving scene to vatch these young stoic faces slowly and silently walking down the runway, everal limping or on crutches. I could not help but feel sorry for them and eflect on the fate of my country.

Once the event was over, we asked to visit the city before leaving. The 'C officials obliged and took us to various famous sites where scars of bomb amages were still in place: the notorious damaged bridge, the bombed hospi-al, the lake young John McCain had parachuted into where he had been cap-ured after his Navy bomber was shot down in 1967. Being the sole Asian face mong the Americans, I was immediately singled out by the inhabitants. They rst took me for Chinese until I talked to them in Vietnamese. By then, wher-ver we walked, I was surrounded by ordinary Vietnamese who were curious to now about the South. They examined my clothing--a green pantsuit; my jew-lry--my engagement diamond ring; and my cameras. I was conscious of being bserved by the guides, who prevented me from asking too many questions. I nevertheless was aware of the poverty around me through these conversations. Stores on the main street, such as they were, were scarce, and almost empty.

It was a memorable day for me, something to brag about with my family when I went back to see them. Unfortunately, that day came much sooner than I expected. We were to be reassigned to Eastern Europe very soon, and I had to go back to see my family for the last time. A month earlier, Malcolm had been expelled from South Vietnam by the government in Saigon because some articles he had written had displeased Thieu. So I would have to go back to Saigon by myself.

Checking my passport, I realized that the North Vietnamese had put an entry stamp into my American passport. When I traveled back to Viet Nam alone, I didn't want an unpleasant incident like the one I had encountered before. So I asked this American immigration officer at that special dinner in Phnom Penh whether I could apply for a new passport. He assured me that it would be no problem.

The next day, I went to see him at the Embassy and presented him with my passport. He asked me to come back in two days. The following day, I received a telephone call to meet him at the hotel reception desk. I went down and there he was with my passport. I beamed.

"I am afraid that I have to keep your passport for a while," he said, bringing me back to earth. "You have violated our law by going to North Viet Nam." He opened my passport at the first page, where were written the names of three restricted countries that we were not allowed to go to -- North Viet Nam, North Korea and Cuba. It was one of the old grey-green passports. Nowadays, the passport is blue and there is no indication of restriction to any country.

The guy had tricked me so as to impound my passport. I asked him to wait and ran up to our room to let Malcolm know. He went down to confront the man. It was no use. Malcolm immediately cabled the New York Times foreign desk. In turn the New York Times called the State Department and filed a complaint. Three days later, the Embassy called to tell me that I was granted a passport for three months, pending an investigation.

"I have never seen an American passport that is only valid for three months," the Vietnamese customs officer said, looking at me with a smile when I went through passport control at Saigon airport. I felt faint and in panic. I weakly smiled back. He stamped the passport and waved me past.

I had paid for being honest. I could have kept my mouth shut and gone home with my old passport. I was sure that the Vietnamese government ould not have even noticed the stamp. Being an American citizen, I might ot have had any problem. It was, nevertheless, a lesson for me about trusting ıe American government or. I its embassy employees too much should have nown by then that the foreign press was not well received by some American mbassy personnel. They did not trust American journalists, and the press did ot trust everything they said. One way for them to get back at Malcolm and ıe New York Times was by punishing me.

Fending for myself when I left Saigon for the United States, I again ın the risk of running amok with authorities on both sides of the Pacific. But ter on, with the help of the New York Times, the State Department decided issue me another passport.

Being a foreign correspondent, Malcolm tried to maintain good relaons with the American Embassy officials responsible for news and information. We met good people and friendly Ambassadors, as well as reluctant or ostile bureaucrats. Later, in Yugoslavia, we had a good friend at the American mbassy who had served a tour in Viet Nam, and he spoke fluent Vietnamese. hen I told him about my miserable passport experience, he humbly offered issue a second passport for me whenever I decided to go back to Viet Nam. ugoslavia was a communist country at the time. True to his words, I went see him in 1975 when South Viet Nam was about to fall. I got the new ıssport within a few hours. All this had taught me a lesson about the imporince of trust. Without it, a simple task in the hands of someone in authority, owever unimportant he might be, could destroy or undo a person's life. And I elieved in honesty and truth -- but, in the case of the American immigration ficer at the embassy in Phnom Penh, I had learned there was sometimes a fine ne between belief and reality.

Malcolm's interviewees: General Vo Nguyen Giap and his wife at their home, His Royal Highness King Norodom Sihanouk, and Henry Kissinger (a,b,c.)

A

B

C

After a failed coup d'état against Bolivian President Torres, we shared a drink with the Russian Tass correspondent and his wife and a Bolivian reporter.

Henry Kissinger in Yugoslavia with President Josip Broz Tito (3a) and with Tito's wife Yovanka, (3b).

A

B

Malcolm relaxes in Buenos Aires by building an airplane kit.

We visited Ushuaia, the southernmost tip of Argentina

Malcolm at the Oruro carnival in Bolivia.

Malcolm with his oxygen bottle, at 5,300 feet on Mount Chacaltaya, altitude 18,000 feet.

The famous Khyber Pass, the border frontier between Pakistan and Afghanistan.

Malcolm and our dog, Nif Naf, at Karachi beach in Pakistan.

A Pathan gun maker shows me a self-made sub machine gun at Darra Adam Khel, a tribal village near Peshawar in Pakistan.

The “Hanoi Hilton,” the prison for American POWs, is seen behind me.

Malcolm in Hanoi during the liberation of the American POWs in 1973.

CHAPTER NINE

Malcolm decided to move to New York at the end of his Eastern Euro-
ean tour of duty in late 1978.

Very often, he made decisions without consulting me. For instance,
uring our last home leave, he had an interview with his chief editor to discuss
ie next move. I had thought that he might want to be assigned to the London
ureau. He came back and told me he had decided on New York. I wanted to
now whether it was his decision or his boss's? It was his own, and he had never
reathed a word about it to me beforehand.

So we moved back to New York, where Malcolm was assigned to cover
ie United Nations. He had occasion to travel with Secretary-General Kurt
Valdheim to North Korea, China, Viet Nam and I think the Philippines or
ndonesia. But he was bored with politics, and asked to be transferred to the
cience News section. There he had a chance to explore and write about as-
onomy, chemistry and other scientific disciplines. He visited such illustrious
boratories as the CERNE in Switzerland and the FEMI Lab in Michigan,
nd watched stars with astronomers in Hawaii and Chile. He wrote brilliant
olumns on science, in simple language that even I and other laymen could
nderstand. I constantly received compliments and praise from friends about
is articles.

And yet, he was unhappy with the New York Times. He never confid-
d in me about his feelings, except when his articles were killed or delayed for
everal days. I had already started to work with the International Rescue Com-
iittee, helping Vietnamese refugees first, followed by Russian Jews, Eastern
uropeans and Africans, mostly Ethiopians and Somalians. I was too preoccu-
ied with my own work to be aware of Malcolm's unhappiness.

"Time Magazine is going to start a new science magazine called Dis-
over, and they are looking for an editor to run it," he casually mentioned over
inner one day. "A girl whom I helped get a job at the New York Times recom-
iended me to them."

"Would you like to?" I was mildly enthusiastic. "You are so much ad-
iired by many readers of what you write. Why do you want to leave for Time
Iagazine?"

"It offers more money and I want to try an editorial position," he smiled sweetly. I was not so sure it would be a good move. “Oh, it’s just thought,” he said.

Typical of Malcolm, the next thing I learned was that he had quit th New York Times and joined the Discover team. He had a big elegant offic on the 15th floor of the Time-Life Building in Rockefeller Center. He starte working later and later every day. One afternoon, as I was having a staff mee ing, he called to let me know that he was in the emergency room because c heart palpitations. I rushed to the hospital, but it was a false alarm. He told m that he had felt faint, and that the Discover manager had called the ambulanc He had never had a hint of any such symptom before.

In three years with Discover, he must have been very unhappy an disappointed. From time to time, he expressed discouragement or complain about his writers, whom he found to be uneducated and incapable.

His only joy was to be able to go back to Antarctica for another visi – his fifth! After he got back, he proposed applying for both of us to spend si months there together. I could take a six-month of leave of absence from m work to be with him. When it turned out that the Antarctica team did not ac cept female civilians under any circumstances, Malcolm dropped the idea – h did not want to be away for six months without me.

“I’ll go crazy if I continue to stay with Discover,” he spilled out hi frustration one spring. “I have an idea for a book. What do you think if I take six-month of leave of absence to write a book? I’ll go to our house in Vermon like I went to Dalat for my first book.”

That was “The New Face of War,” about Viet Nam, contracted b the Bobbs-Merrill publishing house after he received the Pulitzer Prize. H had taken three months’ leave of absence from the Associated Press to seclud himself in Dalat, the vacation resort in Viet Nam, and wanted to repeat thi method with another book in mind.

We had bought the house, in Ascutney, Vermont, during our hom leave before we came back from Eastern Europe. It was one of the reason that Malcolm had decided to go back to work in New York City. It was a coz two-story house, with a huge swimming pool and almost 50 acres of tall ever green trees.

No sooner had we moved in than it became a burglars’ target. As bot of us were working, we used it for long week-ends or summer vacation, an hired an old handy man to take care of it. After several burglaries, we decid ed to pay for security coverage. Despite all our precautions, over eight year it was illegally used as shelter by hunters and the walls and windows wer ddled with shotgun pellets holes. The last straw came one evening when we ceived an urgent telephone call from the security service telling us that their ırveillance camera had shown yet another burglar, braving the snow and cold, alking along our driveway with one of our suitcases. He was caught but, after ine years, we gave up and put the house up for sale. Later, we bought anoth- r one in Thetford, Vermont, adjacent to a beautiful farm. We also added a wimming pool later on.

Malcolm spent six months writing in Ascutney, along with our dog. Vhen I joined him that summer, he looked happy and healthy. He took the ook to his literary agent in New York. He didn't want me to read it and I had o notion what it was about. The book was never published, and Malcolm ever mentioned it again.

Working through his archives, I found a manuscript entitled "Hand's tand," and a letter from his literary agent informing him that he had not ound any publisher interested in his book. I began to read it and tried it on iends in the publishing business. I was told that it was hard for any publisher posthumously accept a manuscript, the reason being the need for editing.

"It's time for me to look for a job. I'll call Abe Rosenthal at the New ork Times," Malcolm told me when he returned to New York, in a tremulous oice that worried me.

"Aren't you going back to Discover?" I asked.

"I've already sent a letter of resignation to them," he said, looking raight at me. "I should never have accepted that job. It was a big mistake. We ave enough savings for several months. I need change, perhaps in the televi- on field. In any case, it's time to go back to work."

"If you are worried about our financial status, I assure you that we are oing all right with my income," I told him. "In any case, with your journalis- c stature, I have no doubt that you could get whatever job you desire." I tried lower his anxiety without hurting his feelings. He didn't say anything but as deep in thought.

After several months of waiting, Malcolm was panicked and concerned. he New York Times offered him a job as Pentagon correspondent in Washing- n. He asked me whether I was willing to move there. Without any hesitation, told him that would be no problem; I could always find another job there. It idn't seem to reassure him. He turned down the job and almost begged Abe to ive him back the job with the Science Section. I was not aware of all the back nd forth communication between Malcolm and the New York Times until I ad his archives after his death.

After a year of doodling at home, he was rehired by The Times. Mal colm must have gone through a long period of uncertainty and despair afte joining the Time Inc. magazine.

I went through his archives before sending them to the Library of Con gress and read the letters exchanged between him and his bosses there. Some c them were combative, and others nasty and insulting. I imagined him fightin on one hand with his writers who did not want to have their copy heavil edited, and on the other hand fighting with his supervisor to let him writ and report on the subjects he knew best. He never shared with me all he ha endured during his time there. I only caught some hints of disagreements wit his superior. I naively took it as natural that such a job required a lot of respon sibility and determination.

The fights might have been the cause of the heart attack. And I ha ignored the signal.

Malcolm went back to the New York Times Science Department o March 28, 1985. I found a torn calendar page on which he wrote "First day o return to Times."

He continued to travel abroad as well as around the country. He cov ered the First Gulf War between 1990 and 1991 at age 60, the oldest reporte on the scene. "What's so moving about finding Browne covering science at th end of his career is the fact that science is in some sense the opposite of wa (everything in life lies somewhere in between)," David Warsh wrote in review ing Malcolm's book "Muddy Boots and Red Socks: A Reporter's Life," in th Boston Sunday Globe on August 29, 1996.

Malcolm was also offered a professorship of Journalism at Princeto University for one year. He worked hard, preparing for the class as well as cor recting homework while he continued covering news for the New York Times He constantly talked about his students and gleefully praised some of them a diligent and intelligent. He had found his vocation.

As he approached 65, he expressed his wish to retire. Unfortunately I was not ready. I was in the prime of my career, receiving federal grants t resettle refugees coming from Albania, Eastern Europe, and Soviet Jews. I addition, we had just bought the new house in Vermont and used up all ou savings. He was disappointed but resigned to having to wait.

One evening, coming home from Brooklyn in a taxi, he drew my at tention by spreading out his two hands in front of me. "It looks like I hav Parkinson's," he muttered.

"It's a sign of aging," I slightly joked although inside, I agreed with his iagnostic.

Two years later, on February 28th, 2000, we both retired. Malcolm ent to see our doctor who, more or less, confirmed our suspicion. He sent im to see a neurologist.

The first few years, we spent most of our springs and summers in our ermont house. We enjoyed its serenity, its pastoral landscape and its constant- changing colors. We took long hikes. We got to know our neighbors and ppreciated the hospitality of our community.

As his Parkinson's rapidly progressed, Malcolm's health deteriorated to ie point that he could neither drive nor walk.

It was in our house in Vermont that Malcolm passed away in October 7, 2012.

CHAPTER TEN

Malcolm's last day, August 27, 2012, had begun, strangely, with a very ood omen. A week before, we had been told that the disease was no longer eatable, and that Malcolm might not last more than two weeks or a month. nd yet, on the 27th, when the nurse came to see Malcolm, he was in a good ood, conversing gaily with her and answering her questions without any hes-ation. The radio was playing one of our favorite pieces of music, the "Rhap-ody on a Theme of Paganini" by Rachmaninoff.

"Would you like me to play this during your funeral?" I calmly asked im, although my heart was wracked with pain.

"No. I prefer Dvorak's String Quartet," he retorted, smiling.

"Which one?" He struggled to remember, but shook his head. I was mazed that we could talk of death, as if we were making plans for a happy trip.

The day seemed to be passing smoothly towards 4 p.m., when Malcolm sked me to put on the DVD of "Final Cut," the last episode of the popular ritish political satire "House of Cards," which we both loved and frequently played when there was nothing of interest on television.

It was a combination of three episodes lumped together. So at 6 p.m., suggested that we should have dinner first and continue later. Malcolm got p by himself, walked to the dining table, and sat down. I served him his vorite dish, chicken pot pie, and he devoured it within a few minutes. I ouldn't believe my eyes. For the last few months, he had been having prob-ms swallowing. The reason was that the muscles in his esophagus had been adly damaged, so much that taking food could cause choking or even death, it went into his lungs. I carefully mashed his food and fed him myself, so to void any risk of his choking. And yet, that evening, without any help, he was ble to eat normally.

After dinner, he got up, by himself, and walked directly to the bath-oom, leaving me standing amazed. Normally, I had to help lift him up from e table, then slowly lead him to the bars along the walls leading to the bath-oom that his brother, Tim, had set up so he could support himself. Also, ormally, I walked with him to the bathroom, prepared his toothbrush and anded it over to him.

I had not recovered from my surprise when Malcolm emerged from the bathroom and demanded to see the rest of the tape.

"I think that you should go to bed and rest," I said, softly, with n conviction.

"No. I am all right," he insisted, moving to the living room and sittin down on his chair, ready for me to turn on the tape.

Silently, we watched. Almost at the dramatic ending, which we bot already knew so well, a familiar sigh came from him, alerting me that he wa in trouble. I rushed to his side, expecting as many times before that he ha fainted. He was stretched out, his arms on the armchair and his legs stretche straight out to the floor. In panic, I called out to him, shook him, tapped on hi cheeks. No answer. I immediately called 911 and within 15 minutes, help ar rived -- two familiar faces, who by now knew all too well what to expect whe they saw Malcolm's inert body. They stretched him out on the floor, and afte I told them what had happened, they started trying to revive him. I expecte him to regain consciousness, as he had many times before, after a few minute But this time, he didn't move.

I realized instantly that he was dying. The paramedics wanted to tr other methods to resuscitate him. I immediately jumped in.

"Please, don't do that," I insisted. I ran to the refrigerator, snatched th non-resuscitation form that the nurse had prepared for us two weeks befor I showed them the paper. They looked at it and stared at me as if to ascertai that that was what I wanted.

It was what Malcolm wanted. He had threatened many times to ki himself if he became incapacitated. In the hospital, the nurse who had fille out the form had also taken care to make sure that it was what he wanted.

Between desperate hope that he would wake up very soon and a feelin of obligation to honor his wishes, I was torn. I looked at him lying there, hardl breathing, his long skinny body and his haggard face full of pain. I had n right to prolong his suffering. I visualized him lying comatose in the hospita waiting for death to come. In tears and despairing, I nodded. The paramedic silently lifted Malcolm to the stretcher and wrapped his frail body, as he re mained unconscious.

It was about 8 p.m. when they carried Malcolm out to the ambulanc I expected it would be a long night. I needed someone to take care of Blondin our cat, and also to watch over the house. I called our neighbors and friend from Germany who had so often witnessed episodes like this and kindly ha given us the support that we needed. Inge Trebitz and her husband, Heinz arrived within 5 minutes. Seeing Malcolm being carried out to the ambulanc ıge suggested she could drive me in her car following the ambulance while leinz stayed in the house. I let Inge lead me to her car. It was an act that often aunted me later, when I kept blaming myself for not being in the ambulance ith Malcolm in case he regained consciousness.

When we arrived at the hospital, we were shown to the room where 1alcolm lay, still unconscious and feebly breathing. A young doctor who was ıere again questioned me about the non-resuscitation form, holding it in his ands. I nodded hopelessly, watching Malcolm's face, expecting him to open is eyes. I called out his name, smoothing his hair, and stroking his cold cheeks. called and called, with the doctor and Inge both closely attentive. A sign of ope came when I saw his lips twisting as if he was trying to speak out. Then e softly breathed out, his chest deflating. The doctor took his pulse and shook is head. He and Inge discreetly left the room, and I was left with Malcolm's ody. I stroked his hair and cheek, numb, no tears, no sound coming from my ıouth. Suddenly, his arm fell, hanging at my side, showing the Rolex watch. hoked with emotion, I took off the watch and laid his arm back on his chest. did it automatically, with a strange feeling that even in death he still cared for ıe. We did not say good-bye.

The doctor came in with someone who asked me whether I had arınged for a funeral home to take Malcolm's body. I had no clue. Fortunately, nge was there, and she asked them to keep Malcolm's body in the morgue vernight so that we could find a funeral home the next day. I kissed Malcolm, nd like a zombie, I followed Inge to the cashier and to her car. She offered to tay with me that night, but I insisted that I wanted to be alone.

The last vision will remain imprinted in my brain until I die: Malolm's last journey, when the ambulance came to carry his listless body to Dartıouth-Hitchcock Hospital in Nashua, New Hampshire.

At his request, Malcolm was buried in our own property in Thetford enter, Vermont. It was a private ceremony, organized with the help of our riends, Heinz and Inge Trebitz. I was fortunate to have members of my family ome from France and California, with Timothy, Malcolm's son, from Canada, nd other close friends and neighbors.

During his illness, we had often discussed his wish to be buried, not remated. Fortunately, there was an old law in Vermont permitting a family to ury a loved one on their own property. All I needed was a permit from the hetford Town Hall.

A week before Malcolm died, (we hadn't expect him to die so soon,) im Masland, the representative of the Cemetery Commission, came to visit us and to inspect the location. Malcolm and I had chosen the highest corne of the property for our graves. Everything seemed to come together without hitch.

I was grateful, during these dark days, that my family and Malcolm were there for me. On the day of his burial, I was in a state of mind tha nothing mattered any more. Guests started to arrive; chairs were put out i a half circle for family members. Speech were made. I sat upright, tearless, i numbness.

When it was time to lower Malcolm's coffin, we gathered around. Ev erybody waited for me to make the first move. I just stood staring at the coffin Heinz took the initiative by scooping up a fistful of dirt and throwing it ont the coffin. My family was staring at me. I took one of the flowers next to m and felt ready to jump down into the grave with it. My paralysis saved m from craziness. My family gently pulled me away. I walked in a fog. I tried t stay calm.

My sister had planted three Peony trees around the grave, to provid shade. Their fragrance, in summer, pleasantly overwhelms the fertilizer in th fields next door. I spent my summer tending the grave and opened up my emo tions, my frustration, and my loneliness to Malcolm's spirit, which, accordin to the Buddhist religion, remains on earth--or so I am told, or so I wish.

Being near him, I feel serene and at peace.

Le Lieu, director of the Refugee Employment Project, with her staff in New York.

Malcolm and Le Lieu Browne in New York.

CHAPTER ELEVEN

Why is it so difficult to write about good, happy memories, incredible dventures and fantastic people?

At present, I sit in front of the window with a pastoral view of green ıeadows and dark forest. It's quiet and serene. Chickadees, goldfinches and tmice perch nearby, and call out for their mates. A hairy woodpecker is busy nocking on the fir tree trunk. A soft summer breeze, from time to time, rustles ırough the willow twigs that graciously wave at its passage. The field beyond as been recently mowed and the hay gathered. A couple of deer with their two ıwns are stomping and gleaning what was left over. The sun peeps through ıe white clouds and shines over the landscape. It is a perfect sleepy summer fternoon.

I think of Malcolm who had dreamt of retiring in Vermont, among the eaceful hills and green meadows, so we could savor the tranquility. Ironically fe is sometime cruel and uncompromising. He was sick throughout those last ıirteen years of his life.

And, here I am in his bedroom, now my study. I stare at the landscape, ıute and thoughtless. I am overwhelmed by the many memories, good and ad, that have boggled my mind when I try to put them in words on paper.

"Under the self-same bough, and heard as there
The birds, the fountains and the ocean hold
Sweet talk in music through the enamored air,
And then a vision on my brain was rolled."
(P.B Shelley- "The triumph of Life.")

I look around me. In addition to the desk and two small bookcases, verything else on the walls or around me has been left untouched. On one all are pictures of the iconic burning monk, the old stone-house where Malolm grew up, the picture of him posing with four other Pulitzer Prizewinners,)avid Halberstam, Peter Arnett, Neil Sheehan and Horst Faas; a certificate of ıembership from the Montagnard Rhade tribe in Viet Nam, and a map of ıntarctica.

On the adjacent wall, a black pirate flag is fully spread out. And below it is a picture of "Alferd" D. Packer, an American prospector convicted o cannibalism in the 19th century, with the typed caption "I never met a man didn't like," dated March 1st, 1874. Another grim and dark picture shows pile of hundreds of human skulls, probably taken at night by Malcolm durin his human-rights reportage on a massacre of Indians in Nicaragua. Yet anoth er gruesome picture shows a pair of torn and bloody human hands hangin among in barbed wire.

These horrific memorabilia invoke the dark side of Malcolm's long ex perience of war, suffering, and death. And now I have inherited his past. W covered the world during our fifty years together. True to his word, he took m along wherever his assignments required his presence, regardless of the extr expense that he personally had to pay for my travel. We were a rare couple. I normal circumstances, foreign correspondents could not afford to take thei spouses or families along for long reporting trips. The divorce rate among cor respondents was high. Malcolm liked to take me with him as often as we coul afford it, almost 90% of his travel. I suppose that, because of his past faile marriages and our brief separation, he truly wanted to share his life with me.

As in any marriage, we had our ups and downs, sometime seriou enough to think of separation and divorce. Nevertheless, we stayed togethe through thick and thin because we recognized our weaknesses as well as ou mistakes. Malcolm was a solid foundation that kept me from hurting myse and our love. Alas! I was guilty of many faults – my childish behavior, m insecurity, my quick temper, my uncontrollable impulses, and my immaturi ty Sometimes a trivial dispute could, in a split second, turn us into morta enemies. On the other hand, I was very sensitive about my race and culture. slight misunderstanding or a mild curse could darken my mood and send m to an uncontrollable rage.

Malcolm could see through me. With his wit, he could spin me an way he wanted. He taunted me when he was upset with his newspaper. Ver often, he made a decision without consulting me.

We covered volcanic eruptions and saw bodies lying on the ground I was cursed by people who did not want to be photographed. In Cambodia we risked being kidnapped by guerrillas. Many photographers and foreign cor respondents for American television had been kidnapped or had disappeare without trace after straying into the enemies' path.

All my problems were mostly minor, and I had the power of the pres behind me. The annoyances I suffered were nothing compared with the per ilous voyages on which the Vietnamese boat people risked their lives to see eedom from tyranny and starvation. I had worked with them and heard the agedies so many of them endured, such as half of a family watching the other alf of their loved ones drifting away at sea, or drowned, or shot. Some parents ever saw their daughters again after Thai pirates kidnapped them to sell as sex aves. Even when they were safe in a new country, these refugees faced discrim- ıation, depression and suicide attempts.

My life with Malcolm was romantic and fascinating, for both of us. Jnlike tourists who spend a few days visiting famous spots, we were given chance to connect with the inhabitants and learn about their history. We ppreciated the beauty of the places we covered, and the friendly and warm na- ves we encountered. We learned their language and their culture. We savored ıeir exotic and delicate culinary dishes. But because we were there to report n war and politics, we were consciously looking for the ugly side of human ature. We dug up human sufferance and injustice. Malcolm's responsibility 'as to report objectively what he had witnessed or what people told him had appened. It might make an impact on the American society and government, r it might be regarded as a tale of some remote country that had no conse- uences on the American life.

In one of his low moments, Malcolm wrote: "The greatest of the hu- ıan spirit is less in succeeding than in raising a fist against the impossible." eing a foreign correspondent in the 20th century was prestigious and priv- eged. Landing in a remote country such as Pakistan or Afghanistan or even olivia was, for us, like landing on an alien planet. People stared at us while we 'ere awed by their exotic costumes and mystified by a language that we could either read, nor speak. We were free to go anywhere we liked. Military officers nd government dignitaries openly welcomed us. We felt that we were in a ›ecial class. Despite being expelled from autocratic countries or harassed by ecret services, we were never physically harmed or intentionally manhandled ı purpose. I have watched television reporters in the 21st century with appre- ension, especially when freedom of the press was the topic. Malcolm believed ıat foreign correspondents were a dying species, something I have also read in n article. The world has "lost its mysteries", he thought.

Personally, my life was built on an accident I had never anticipated. did not expect to be the wife of a foreign correspondent who would love nd care for me. I saw the world when civility and respect were still valued verywhere, when air travel was exciting and inspirational, the earth was less opulated and there was more space for individuality and imagination. All our ls nowadays are born of overpopulation, poverty and greed. When I returned

to Saigon in December of 2016, I hardly recognized the "Pearl of the Orient
that I used to know. Its population had jumped from 2 million in 1975 to ove
10 million. Pollution, noise and traffic deadened the city.

I owed everything to my lucky star and Malcolm's love.

Darling, life is too short.
We are whisked away
On a TGV train
Fast, exhilarating, absorbing
In luxurious comfort,
Shuttled through memory lane.
Beautiful passages, painful
Climbing, but no crash.
Smooth, smoothly we roll
High and low, together,
Always together.
Aches and pains are
Our toll.
But our spirits remain
Forever
Young and loving.

ACKNOWLEDGMENTS

I would like to express my gratitude and profound appreciation to my earest friends who have been the engine that drove me to write. I owe the xistence of this manuscript to the generosity, kindness and love these friends ave bestowed on me.

Linda Laundry initiated the idea. She never gave up believing in me nd in my capability as a writer.

John Sanborn is my mentor and teacher. He has given much time to ounsel me, and followed and edited my writing at every step.

Without Linda and John, the memoir would never have materialized.

Michelle Sherburne helped with correspondence and created the textual arrangement for the book.

Craig R. Whitney, former foreign correspondent and editor for the **New York Times**, an old friend, went through the final draft of the manuscript, and helped me find a way to publish it.

Jonathon Wolfer arranged for the publication of my book, and esigned the cover and the interior layout and typography. He is himself published author.

ABOUT THE AUTHOR

Le Lieu Browne, a native of Vietnam, began her career with the Minister of Information of the Republic of South Vietnam, went on to work with Radio Australia, the United States Information Service and with her husband, Malcolm Browne as a Photographer and Journalist bringing them around the globe covering world events for the New York Times. Le Lieu retired as the project General Manager of the New York City Refugee Employment Project after twenty years of service. She splits her time between New York City and Vermont. This is her first book.

Made in United States
North Haven, CT
03 January 2022